THE METHUEN DRAMA BOOK OF MODERN MONOLOGUES FOR MEN: TEENS TO THIRTIES

T0333664

THE METHUEN DRAMA BOOK OF MODERN MONOLOGUES FOR MEN: TEENS TO THIRTIES

Edited by Dee Cannon

methuen | drama

LONDON • NEW YORK • OXFORD • NEW DELHI • SYDNEY

METHUEN DRAMA
Bloomsbury Publishing Plc
50 Bedford Square, London, WC1B 3DP, UK
1385 Broadway, New York, NY 10018, USA
29 Earlsfort Terrace, Dublin 2, Ireland

BLOOMSBURY, METHUEN DRAMA and the Methuen Drama logo
are trademarks of Bloomsbury Publishing Plc

First published in Great Britain by Oberon Books 2016
This edition published by Methuen Drama 2022
Reprinted 2024

Compilation copyright © Dee Cannon, 2016

Foreword copyright © Tom Hiddleston, 2016

Dee Cannon has asserted her right under the Copyright,
Designs and Patents Act, 1988, to be identified as author of this work.

Designed by Konstantinos Vasdekis

All rights reserved. No part of this publication may be reproduced or
transmitted in any form or by any means, electronic or mechanical,
including photocopying, recording, or any information storage or retrieval
system, without prior permission in writing from the publishers.

Every effort has been made to trace copyright holders and to obtain
their permission for the use of copyright material. The publisher
apologizes for any errors or omissions and would be grateful if notified
of any corrections that should be incorporated in future reprints or
editions of this book.

Bloomsbury Publishing Plc does not have any control over, or
responsibility for, any third-party websites referred to or in this book. All
internet addresses given in this book were correct at the time of going
to press. The author and publisher regret any inconvenience caused if
addresses have changed or sites have ceased to exist, but can accept no
responsibility for any such changes.

All rights whatsoever in this play are strictly reserved and
application for performance etc. should be made before rehearsal
to the authors' agents. No performance may be given
unless a licence has been obtained.

A catalogue record for this book is available from the British Library.

A catalog record for this book is available from the Library of Congress.

ISBN: PB: 978-1-3502-7546-1
ePub: 978-1-7831-9938-9

Printed and bound in Great Britain

eBook conversion by Lapiz Digital Services, India.

To find out more about our authors and books visit www.bloomsbury.com
and sign up for our newsletters.

To my students,
past, present and future.

CONTENTS

Men 20s

Men 30s

Foreword by Tom Hiddleston

If you're reading these words, and you've found this book, chances are you want to be an actor. Being an actor isn't easy – your job is to convince people that you're someone else – but the challenge and the joy of being an actor is to be found in the work that you do to make it look easy.

If you're picking a monologue from this book, let me start by saying this: you're already on your way. You're already an actor. You have already committed. You bought this book. And that's all you have to keep doing: commit. Commit with everything you have, commit with all your heart and soul, and you'll get where you want to go.

People often ask me for advice. I'm always wary of giving it. We like to find our own way in life and, by and large, most of us do – some of us take longer detours than others – but we all get there in the end.

We all have within us limitless possibility.
We're born with it: the capacity to be anyone or anything.
Acting is a craft that plays on that sense of possibility – the potential of every man and woman to feel and express the depth and breadth of what it means to be alive – in all our joy and pain, our virtue and vulnerability, our weakness and our wisdom.

I trained with Dee Cannon at the Royal Academy of Dramatic Art from 2002-2005. I remember her acting classes as spaces of emotional freedom and technical discipline. She challenged us as students to be fearless and precise in our explorations and expressions of emotional truth. Whether we were working on Shakespeare or Sam Shepard, Pinter or Pirandello, emotional truth was paramount. It was from her that I learned that the truth can sometimes be surprising. The truth doesn't have to be serious and heavy – it can often be very funny. Any character can turn from dark to light on a dime. In life, people laugh as often as they cry. Sometimes they laugh when they feel like they should be crying. Sometimes they laugh and cry at the same time.

Whatever monologue you choose, whatever you want your monologue to express – be truthful. Be honest. Be open. Be brave. Don't force it. Trust your gut. Your gut will tell you if it doesn't feel right. If you believe it, they'll believe it. That's the hardest part, and at the same time the simplest part, of being an actor. Believe it. Commit to that belief, commit to your imagination. And you'll soar.

I'll leave you with three pieces of advice I've inherited from minds finer than my own:

In Hamlet's speech to the players, Shakespeare gives some of the greatest acting advice of all time:

"Speak the speech, I pray you, as I pronounced it to
you, trippingly on the tongue...

　　　　　　　　　　　　　　... Nor do not saw the air
too much with your hand, thus. But use all gently.
For in the very torrent, tempest, and, as I may say,
the whirlwind of passion, you must acquire and beget
a temperance that may give it smoothness...
Be not too tame neither. But let your own discretion
be your tutor. Suit the action to the word, the
word to the action, with this special observance,
that you o'erstep not the modesty of nature.
For any thing so overdone is from the purpose of playing,
whose end, both at the first and now, was and is, to hold, as 'twere,
the mirror up to nature, to show virtue her own feature,
scorn her own image, and the very age and body of
the time his form and pressure".

Or, in the words of the great Marlon Brando, to whom all actors working today owe an immeasurable debt:

"Everything that you do – make it as real as you can. Make it alive. Make it tangible. Find the truth of that moment".

The great acting teacher Stella Adler, who trained Brando, once said:

"Life beats down and crushes the soul, and art reminds you that you have one".

Your job as an actor is to bare it.

Go get 'em.

Tom Hiddleston, 2016

Introduction

I have been working with actors over many years and it goes without saying that at some point in your career you will be required to find and prepare a monologue – whether that's for getting into drama school, a 3rd year showcase, a professional monologue slam or auditioning for a theatre company or agent, your search for that perfect monologue is on. It can feel overwhelming at times to wade through plays and/or various monologue books. How do you know what suits you? Should you go for something meaty, dramatic or comedic?

It is indeed an arduous task at times but I believe if you follow a few simple guidelines this should help you in your quest for the ideal speech.

HOW TO CHOOSE AND WORK ON SPEECHES

It helps greatly if the piece is age appropriate. You should find a truthful and emotional connection. You need to separate what you 'like' and what 'suits you.' These are two different things. You also need to understand you're showcasing your talent and abilities to professionals or an audience who often haven't seen you perform before; therefore, you should choose to your strength and not your weakness.

However unnatural this process feels, it is your responsibility to bring the speech alive and find the truth and through-line of the character – that means having empathy and not judging or commenting on your character's circumstance.

It is not just a question of learning the lines. You should start with sourcing and reading the play. If need be, do some research – write a back-story if you have time. Look up any words you don't know. Find out the correct pronunciation if the word is unfamiliar to you. Work out who you are, where you are and who you're speaking to. You can decide if the speech works best sitting down or standing up. There's no right or wrong. If sitting – set a chair in place of the person you're talking to. If standing, work out where the other person is sitting or standing.

Don't feel you have to restrict yourself to just your age section. If you find something in another category that suits you – and you connect to – choose it based on the content and not the age bracket.

Also if you like a speech and it's too long, feel free to cut and adapt it in order to meet your needs. The same applies to speeches that are set in another country or region – it doesn't necessarily mean that you have to do them in that accent – therefore don't feel bound or obliged to do so. You can cut or alter references in order to accommodate your culture as long as you don't change the heart and main objective of the speech.

When you're performing, be careful your nerves don't take hold of you and make you blurt out the speech. Take a moment and breathe deeply, trust that all the good work you've done prior has not evaporated. When you're auditioning, be it for drama school, an actors' showcase or anywhere else, you need to create the world of the character; once you have done that, you need to own it, which in turn will involve and transport the panel or audience. You should aim to be truthfully connected and have a clear thought process with specific intentions.

NEW FORMAT

I am a passionate believer in applying technique to text, therefore I am proud to introduce my new format monologue books by providing a work page alongside the text in order for you to make your actor's notes and to 'Action' your speech as illustrated in my acting book *In-Depth Acting*. This means you no longer have to write all over the monologue or on a separate notebook or even on scraps of paper. Here you can neatly work out 'Objectives,' thoughts and 'Transitive Verbs' adjacent to the text, which I hope will make your process much easier.

IN CONCLUSION

I have endeavoured to choose carefully a diverse selection of monologues from the wonderful plays of Oberon Books. Try to have fun in the process, it doesn't always have to be an arduous task – remember it's important to find something that you like, that best suits your experience and that overall you can relate to. Commitment, passion and hard work go a long way.

I really enjoyed compiling and editing these speeches so I hope you will find the selection inspiring, interesting and challenging.

Please note that some of the extracts have been edited for audition/showcase purposes and will therefore slightly differ from the text as originally published.

TEENS

BOTTLENECK
by Luke Barnes

Bottleneck premiered as part of the 2012 Edinburgh Festival. The production transferred to Soho Theatre London and then toured theatres across the UK. A revival production of the play took place at Edinburgh Festival in July 2014.

The play is set in Liverpool, 1989, and features only one character, Greg, who is thirteen. He has just started secondary school. He earns pocket money sweeping up hair in a barber's. Girls are aliens. Liverpool FC are everything. It's written in quite a strong Liverpudlian dialect which can be modified if need be.

In this first piece Greg is mouthing off about his Dad, primarily because Greg has just been given free tickets to see his beloved Liverpool team but as his father believes he shouldn't get anything for nothing, he takes him down to his friend's barber shop to earn some money. Greg has a laugh at his father's expense on his first day.

GREG – 13 (LIVERPOOL)

My Dad's a hypocrite because he's not looking after me when he goes out is he? Does that mean I don't matter? Don't care anyway. I'm not going to wash tonight. I'm going to bed. Just because he thinks I should doesn't mean it's true.

He's got all moral since mum left. He says 'when we die, she'll be in hell so I'm doing everything possible to get into heaven.'

When I get in from school he's got it all sorted. He's got me a job in 'is mate's barber's and he marches me around holding my hand. It's gay.

We get there and it's this big bald guy with loads of magazines with tits in everywhere and he keeps me there for 4 hours. 4 hours 'e keeps iz 'airdressers open til ten. 4 hours! I sweep up 'air. Ginger hair, black hair, grey hair, beard hair, muzzie hair you name it and I sweep it up. It's disgusting. 'e goes the toilet do you know I do? I pick up this big bit of black 'air, like mine, and I get some glue ... and I ... glue ... the hair to my face, like this, to make it look like a muzzie and go 'Look mister

Notes

I look like me Dad don't I. Then I take Dad's mate's aviators and run around shooting people that walk past going 'I AM JOHN MCCLANE I AM JOHN MCCLANE, LOOK AT ME YIPPEE KI YAY MOTHER FUCKER.' Next thing I know I'm outside and it's cold. I'm not allowed back. BUT I've got 3 quid. Which means I'm 3 quid closer to my 14.50 for the footy tickets.

Can't believe I have to pay for the tickets.

Notes

BOTTLENECK
by Luke Barnes

Bottleneck premiered as part of the 2012 Edinburgh Festival. The production transferred to Soho Theatre London and then toured theatres across the UK. A revival production of the play took place at Edinburgh Festival in July 2014.

The play is set in Liverpool, 1989, and features only one character, Greg, who is thirteen. He has just started secondary school. He earns pocket money sweeping up hair in a barber's. Girls are aliens. Liverpool FC are everything. It's written in quite a strong Liverpudlian dialect which can be modified if need be.

Greg and his new best mate Tom are walking home and his friend decides to suddenly hurl a rock through a police car's window. They both run off but one of the policemen catches up with Greg and drives him back home to explain himself in front of his dad.

GREG – 13 (LIVERPOOL)

So I'm sitting in the back of this car and it stinks of piss. I ask the fella 'Hey mate, why does it smell of piss in the back of your pussy wagon?' and 'e goes 'firstly it's not a pussy wagon, it's a police car and secondly a homeless lady pissed herself there this morning, haven't had time to wash it yet'... 'wa? So I'm sitting on homeless lady piss?' 'should have thought about that before you started being a smart arse shouldn't ya'. Fucking hell. If I'd known that I would just bought a pasty and gone 'ome ... Fuck Tom for getting away. I didn't even do anything.

As we drive past everyone's drawing the curtains. It's dead quite. Like dead quite. And we pull up to ours and I can see Dad in the window. Looking. Fuck. 'E looks dead grey. Dead solemn. I get out, am not handcuffed or anything ... I could run away ... Should I? The bussie looks at me, 'e knows. I make my mind up not to, probably better. And they knock on the door. And Dad answers.

And I go in to the sitting room and sit in silence. I don't hear the rest of the conversation. I take it Dad doesn't like this policeman.

Notes

'E turns and 'is face is red. He takes his belt off and for a second I think he's going to do what Tom's Dad did to him and show me his cock. But he doesn't. He takes off his belt and he twats me with it. Not on my arse like last time but everywhere. All over me body. All over me face. Me arms. Me legs. And it fucking hurts. It's like he's had all this rage bottled up in him about mum and Collin and all these things and they've just boiled up inside him and he's let it all out. All over me. And it hurts. Fuck you Dad. He opens his cabinet, takes something in a bag out and goes up to his room locking it behind him. I stand there. Can feel the rage bubbling up inside me, all that work for nothing. I'm fucked off. I fucking hate my Dad. I didn't even throw the fucking rock. I feel so fucking angry.

Notes

THE KEEPERS OF INFINITE SPACE
by Omar El-Khairy

The Keepers of Infinite Space *had its world premiere at Park Theatre in January 2014.*

A play about a Palestinian prisoner in an Israeli jail. It explores the dynamics of the Israeli prison system revealing the painful complexities of the Israeli-Palestinian conflict.

Shadi is a sixteen-year-old Palestinian prisoner. Tom works for the British International Committee of the Red Cross as an aid worker. He is trying to convince Shadi to record his testimony upon arrest.

SHADI – 16 (PALESTINIAN)

(Beat.) I hung in the air – blood dripping from my body. My shirt covered in blood. My whole body shaking. I remember feeling numb – from the shrapnel that hit me in the thigh.

We were at this demonstration. My brother, Abed – he was – was standing right next to me. I'd told him not to come, but he wouldn't listen.

He was hit straight in the head with a tear-gas canister.

'There is no change nor strength except through Allah, to Allah we belong, and to Him we will return.'

That's all I remember him saying – my father.

Pause.

It was sometime in the morning – three – four, maybe. I heard this loud bang – then the sudden stench of gas. There was a flood of soldiers into the house. My mother began shouting, and then I felt someone grab me and rip me out of bed. The soldiers took me outside – to their jeep. My mother followed them – lashing out and screaming. *(Beat.)* But my father – he just stood there – in the doorway. Silent.

That's the last time I saw them.

Pause.

I was undressed and left standing in my underwear. They dragged me for interrogation. They beat me. They beat you hard in those first few days because they know no one's going to see you – or the bruises. And this carried on for days.

Notes

I don't really know how long. Question after question. I was real hungry – starving. I told them, but they just said I could eat once I'd confessed.

They put me in this room. It kept going from hot to cold – freezing to boiling. I don't know how they did it. Then, after a few hours, I started to feel my heart beating faster and faster. I shouted for them to let me out. Nothing. I thought my heart was going to explode at any moment.

A few days later they showed me this video of children throwing stones at soldiers – and – *(Beat.)* And I admitted – that I was one of them. One of the kids in the video.

It wasn't me though – in the video.

I just had to – you know.

Pause.

(Beat.) And what are you going to do with that testimony, Tom? *(Beat.)* Give it to your superiors?

(Beat.) And what do you think they're going to do with it?

(Beat.) You're just wasting your time, my friend.

Notes

SOME PEOPLE TALK ABOUT VIOLENCE
by Lulu Raczka and Barrel Organ

Some People Talk About Violence was first presented by Barrel Organ at Summerhall at the Edinburgh Fringe Festival 2015 and subsequently transferred to Camden People's Theatre.

The play deals with a girl suffering from acute depression. She recently lost yet another job and now rarely leaves her home; instead she obsesses over the TV show The Big Bang Theory. *We learn very early on in the play that she's done something that has led to her arrest. The story unfolds through a narrator, her mother and brother. When his sister phones him from prison, her brother immediately returns from Thailand, where he lives with his boyfriend.*

Here, the brother recounts the time when he and his sister were kids and invented a story about a door in their house that led to 'the secret children'.

THE BROTHER – TEENS/LATE TEENS* (UK)

There was this one thing that we always had – Me and my sister –

When we were little kids –

This really stupid joke –

It seems weird to explain it now –

You know – to actually explain the stupid

things you thought as kids – when you're an adult –

There were these marks in our wall – In the flat we grew up in –

Marks that came up from the floor – In the wall of our living room –

and made like a rectangle on the wall –

About our height as kids – And I said it was like a door for kids –

And then we used to joke around for ages –

About how we could get through the door – And where the door went –

And all that stuff –

* Older in the play but can be played younger.

Notes

And this one time –

She said –

That's where the secret children live –

And I remember it really clearly because up till then I'd been laughing and suddenly I was fucking terrified –

And she just said yeah –

It's where the secret children live –

Mum's secret children –

And from that point on we were obsessed –

So the way we saw it mum had these secret children –

A little boy and a little girl like us –

And everyday when we went to school they came out of the wall –

And they replaced us – And the thing is –

They didn't have to go to school cause they were better than us –

They already knew all the stuff at school –

And whenever we ate dinner –

This was when mum would get pissed off at us –

Cause we'd whisper to each other about what they would've had for dinner –

The secret children –

But in the morning they would have had this great dinner –

And we'd describe it to each other –

Always so much better than our dinner –

Mum would get annoyed –

Cause she'd never know what was going on – Cause we'd be there laughing and whispering – And sometimes she'd try to be part of the joke – But it never really worked –

She never could be part of the joke –

Cause she didn't know what the joke was – Maybe she'd be upset by it if I told her now – Maybe she'd think we were being rude –

That in some way it was about how we didn't feel like she did enough for us –

But it really wasn't like that at all –

Notes

See me and my sister –

In a lot of ways we aren't close –

She won't know the little things – you know?

She won't know my hair cut – or what music I'm listening to but she –

And I don't know how to put it without it sounding stupid –

But she gets me –

On the phone – when she called me – she said this one word –

And thinking about it –

I dunno –

I –

She broke into someone else's house –

She waited in their bathroom for them to come home –

And that was all in the name of becoming a –

As I say about us being close – I get it –

I get why she would do that –

Notes

CHALK FARM

by Kieran Hurley and AJ Taudevin

Chalk Farm was written for A Play, a Pie, and a Pint at Oran Mor in Glasgow in September 2012 and was presented in a production by ThickSkin at the Edinburgh Fringe in 2013, before touring internationally.

The play's backdrop is the 2011 London riots, as witnessed by a mother and son who have recently moved into their new high-rise Chalk Farm council estate.

Here, Jamie is marvelling and musing about life from such a high vantage point.

JAMIE – 14 (UK)

I used to love it, just staring out that window. Like a watchtower. Like I do now, up on the roof. But it started with me and mum, at that window. Just staring out, like you could keep an eye on things for everyone if you wanted to. I would sit there at night-time just watching. And I know it's corny but the times when I was watching with mum those was the best times of all. Back before her face was tripping her all day and she used to like, I don't know, smile sometimes and shit. When I was like a kid you know? We'd sit there just watching out for all the people down below. We even saw 7/7 from up here, me and mum watching all the madness and disaster from the window.

7/7 and I was like 7. 777. Ha. Wicked. You know how 666 is the code for the devil? Well maybe like 777 is the code for like, I don't know, like whoever the opposite of the devil is. Like, angels and shit. But, like, cool angels. Watchtower angels. Hero angels. Like a cross between Batman and angels. Bat Angels. Bat Angels what can look out their windows and be like calling out 'Be careful, people of Chalk Farm! There's like smoke and bombs and fire and shit. You grannies and granddads and babies and, like, old people, you should all stay at home where it's safe and have a nice cup of tea until we tell you it's all over. Don't worry, we got you covered. 'Cause we can see it all, yeah? All of it. The whole city. Watching out for you, like keeping it safe.' Like Bat Angels!

Notes

Me and mum don't do that sort of stuff these days. Whenever she's in, I'm like front door, bedroom, in and out. She's giving me all that. She wants it to be always like it was when I was a kid. And I can't be doing with it. Life's just not like that. And anyway, the people down there don't know that you're looking out for them. They don't look up here. They don't notice. Nobody looks up at Chalcots and thinks, there's Jamie and his mum keeping a look out for us. Thanks Bat Angels! Nah. Nobody gives a shit. Nobody even looks up here. Ever.

Notes

CHALK FARM
by Kieran Hurley and AJ Taudevin

Chalk Farm was written for A Play, a Pie, and a Pint at Oran Mor in Glasgow in September 2012 and was presented in a production by ThickSkin at the Edinburgh Fringe in 2013, before touring internationally.

The play's backdrop is the 2011 London riots, as witnessed by a mother and son who have recently moved into their new high-rise Chalk Farm council estate.

Here, Jamie is marvelling and musing about life from such a high vantage point.

JAMIE – 14 (UK)

So we head down to the tube and there's this big gang proper kickin in the bike shop. But there's smoke and light from further down the high street and so Junior points and says 'Fuck the bikes let's get down there' and so we run towards the light and noise, the two of us running, and Junior's giving it 'This is history Jamie, this is history being written tonight!'

And we get there and there's crowds all standing around the Sainsbury's and there is like mad electricity in the air, and in their eyes, everyone all totally buzzing, like wired. Like never seen nothing like it, and the street looks familiar and different all at the same time. And they're all holding bricks. All these people, kids with bricks, and older geezers too. All holding bricks. And I know it's stupid yeah but I'm thinking it's like Lego. Like Lego innit.

And I'm laughing 'cause it's all kicking off and –

Fucking BAM! There's this sharp shattering crash as a brick flies through the Sainsbury's window and the crowd all rush like ants towards it. There is this loud crackling noise like frying bacon and a bunch of kids are peeling the smashed window away like big strips of sunburnt skin. And suddenly before I've even got time to catch up with myself, I'm running in there with them, and it's almost like I'm watching myself do it, like it's not real.

And I'm watching myself running inside and I'm shouting

Notes

'Brap brap brap' like everyone else, jumping about, hood up, and I've got this big smile on my face, and my eyes are wired and electric like everyone's are, and I don't really know why but it all feels fucking amazing.

Like a rush, like exciting, yeah?

And people are running about crazy like filling up shopping trolleys full of all sorts of shit, like crisps, like bread, like fucking washing powder. And suddenly I'm not outside watching myself running in and jumping and smiling and shouting. I'm inside and I'm stood still staring at this big shiny stand lined with bottles of fizzy pink wine. And I'm thinking about mum. And I'm thinking about how I can't remember the last time I seen her properly smile. How I don't even see her no more. And in my head I can see her with her big round smiling cheeks, drinking that pink fizz and I'm thinking about how that would make her happy. A treat. Like a treat, you know? And I'm thinking: I can just take it. I can just actual take it.

And the next thing you know there is this big fucking fire catching outside the shop, so I look around and grab one of the bottles that survived the smash so mum can still get her treat, and we run off through the fire practically, bursting through the flames like the Hulk only my skin's probably pink not green 'cause of all the fizz.

And we set off up the high street stinking of smoke and laughing and I stick my headphones in and we run, me with a bottle of pink fizz in my left hand and Junior tossing this broken cash register drawer up in the air and catching it like a trophy and laughing. 'Oi,' he says 'Jamie! Catch!' Fucking jokes man.

Coming round the bend to the bike shop only there's cops there now, lines and lines of armoured cops and you can see they're moving in on the crowd and people are shouting calling them murderers.

But there's no fucking way they're getting my mum's treat. And I stop there, on the street corner, near the bike shop. Clothes stinking of smoke. All sticky and sweet and stained from the pink fizz. And the iPod is set to shuffle, and it starts playing this well slow song. This slow, cheesy song that my mum likes.

Notes

And I stand still. And I feel like everything is slowing down under the watchful eye of Chalcots Estate. I know that if I was up there, a Bat Angel, looking down on the city I'd be able to see me. Standing there on a street corner at this huge crack in the world, my world, while all around me London burns. I can see me. They can see me. They're gonna have to take fucking notice now.

And I'm looking around at the row of cops, the mob, the smashed glass, the surface ripped open, the stains, the stink of smoke, the sign from the tube floating above it all saying: Chalk Farm.

And I'm thinking: this is it. This is it. It doesn't get better than this.

Notes

VIOLENCE AND SON
by Gary Owen

Violence and Son *was first presented at the Royal Court Jerwood Theatre Upstairs, Sloane Square, on 3 June 2015.*

The play is set in a small town in South Wales and deals with violence, love and loss. Liam is still grieving the loss of his mother. His father is a violent drunk and they both seem to enjoy winding each other up. Liam, an avid Dr Who fan, brings home Jen; both are on a high from a Dr Who convention. He really likes her but she has a boyfriend and his father's uncouth behavior doesn't help matters.

It's late and Jen is staying the night. Liam has unsuccessfully tried to convince her to be his girlfriend. Feeling sad, he uncharacteristically opens up to Jen about how much he misses his mother.

Please note Liam doesn't have a Welsh accent.

LIAM – TEENS (UK)

I think about it all the time. I think – how long now till she comes through the door and takes me home? You know you get pins and needles? Say in your leg. And you can't walk. But you don't really worry about it because, you know it'll go and you'll be fine in a minute? This is like that. I'm not worried cos, it'll be fine, in a minute. Cos like, if my mum died but she was a bitch, I wouldn't mind so much? She was nice. I mean, probably since I was thirteen I slightly thought she was a twat but, after getting the diagnosis and then the surgery and the chemo and then, when it became clear she was really going to die, I probably, some point in that process, started to see her good points, quite a lot more than I had. No I don't miss her. Why would I miss her? She's coming to get me any second. Listen, that's her. Here she is – Which means you don't need to worry about me. Or feel guilty. Or make an effort to be nice, or do anything. You definitely don't have to be with me, if actually you want to be with your boyfriend.

You know you're supposed to go through these stages. When you know you're gonna die? Like … anger, denial, pathetic last minute embrace of religion, then acceptance. You accept you're gonna die. It just means you, accept that you're dying. You accept, the life you got, was what you got, and you stop

Notes

wishing there was more. You're just grateful for what there was. There's not a trick. It's just literally, accepting.

And stopping fighting. And stopping struggling. And when you stop struggling, you can find a bit of peace. *(Beat.)* My mum never got to there. Because of me. Because she knew she was leaving me, with no-one. So she kept fighting, right to the end. She hated herself for dying. D'you see? Her last seconds. There was no peace. No calm. None of that for her. Just – despair. Because of me. Because she was leaving me behind. *(Beat.)* So you see I've been loved. I know what it is. And you –

Notes

WHOLE
by Philip Osment

This play was inspired by real interviews and conversations as well as drama-based workshops facilitated by 20 Stories High, a company that specializes in imaginative theatre for young people aged between 13 and 30.

Whole *is a play about four South East London kids in their late teens reliving and acting out a story from when they were younger; a story about their lost friend Holly.*

Dylan, unemployed, talks about a single event when he was bullied – his school friends suspected him of being 'Gay.'

DYLAN – 19, PLAYING HIMSELF AT 15 (UK)

It was on my way back from school. Joseph had gone in the shop – he was going to catch me up. I was coming up to the railway bridge and I saw them up there hanging around looking at the trains. There was five of them – three boys from Year Eleven and two from my year – Flakey Blake and Ashley. Chavs. When I saw them I thought of going a different way but it would have meant going back to the main road and that's much longer. When I came up the steps they went quiet and Ashley said something to one of the older boys and they were looking at me and smiling and I thought, 'Something's going to go off.' But I didn't think anything bad would happen. They were standing in my way so I had to push past them and they said, 'Oooh, he thinks he's hard, he thinks he's hard!' Then one of them said, 'Wait up!' like quite friendly and I looked round. That was my mistake – you should never look them in the eyes. He said, 'Is it true?' and I said, 'Is what true?' and he said, 'Your friend Holly says you're gay!' And I said, 'Piss off!' – something like that and they went, 'Ooooohhh tough guy!' and by that time they'd got round the other side of me and I felt someone going in my bag and I pulled away but he had my Corinne Bailey CD and he was going, 'Who's this? She your gash, Dilys?' And someone else said, 'Dilys don't go in for gash. You're queer and we're going to shank you Dilys.'

Notes

Stuff like that. And I'm trying to get my CD back because I thought, 'You're not getting that, my Mum just bought me that.' And they were holding it up so I couldn't reach it. And then, and then, then this guy from year 11 – he's really fat and sly – he throws the CD over the side of the bridge and it goes down on the track and the others are laughing and flicking their fingers like they can't believe he did it. And they were looking at me to see what I would do. Anyway then Joseph came up and they went quiet. And Flakey said, 'Hi Joseph!' like all normal and Joseph said, 'Hi' and they started talking about football because Joseph's a bit of a star player at school. Anyway so they just went off and they were like sniggering and the fat one said like out of the side of his mouth, 'You gonna slip it to him when you get home, Joseph?' I don't know if Joseph heard that but he must have seen what was happening. But we just carried on walking. We didn't say anything about it. It was like it hadn't happened. It was like – I don't know – it was like a dirty secret. I wasn't going to tell a teacher or anything. I'm not a snitch. And I certainly wasn't going to tell my Mum because I knew she'd go up the school and make a fuss. And anyway she'd start asking why Holly was saying that about me. Holly was the only person I might have talked to about it. But seeing as it had come from her … I knew it must have come from her … she'd been blanking me ever since she'd seen me and Chantal down the graveyard … I just felt like there was nobody I could talk to about it.

Notes

SOLOMON AND MARION
by Lara Foot Newton

Solomon and Marion *was first presented by the Baxter Theatre Centre at the University of Cape Town in November 2011.*

The play is set somewhere near Port Alfred, Eastern Cape, in 2009, the year before the soccer World Cup in South Africa – an event which South Africans see as the answer to all their transport, crime and poverty issues.

A two-hander. Solomon turns up at the house of Marion Banning, a South African older lady of English heritage. He befriends her before he reveals who he is and makes his confession. Solomon is described as inquisitive, aloof and fragile.

SOLOMON – 19 (BLACK/SOUTH AFRICAN)

I was there when Jonathan was killed.

He often bought me sweets ...

Douglass, Sticks and Arthur, these were the older boys my grandmother told me not to be with, they made me to stand behind Jonathan at the machine. I got his number. 56547.

The boys had been drinking all day and smoking Tik Tik.

That afternoon they made me to stand on the side of the road. The dust road that takes you to the highway. They made me to stop him ... Jonathan saw me and pulled to the side.

I thought they just wanted his card. The boys from the gang were hiding in the bushes,

Douglass had a gun. A real gun. I didn't know that. It was my first time to see this gun.

I started to cry, to beg them. Arthur gave me a klap[1]... there was blood.

They made him stop the car next to the scrap yard,

'Hey, take off your pants, take off your trousers. *(Laughing and jeering.)* And your shoes, your shoes! Tie him wena, tie him.'

They tied his hands behind his back with plastic that you find oranges in. Jonathan was making sounds like drowning – he was crying – I saw he pissed his pants ...

Notes

Douglass screamed at me! 'Vok off you stabane,[2] if you tell anyone I will kill you and all of your family! Voetsak![3]'

As I turned to go, Jonathan said something to me. It was a message for you. That is why I am here. That is why I have been coming here, to give you the message.

He said: 'Solomon, please tell my mother, I wasn't scared.'

And then, I turned and ran. *(Pause.)* And then I heard the shot.

I was only a small boy. I was twelve years old. They had many friends. If I had said something they would have sent their friends to kill me. Hang me, or burn me, or rape my sister or even my grandmother. They are like dogs that take the meat from the table. They feel nothing. And anyway one year later, Douglass was shot by the police during a robbery at a supermarket. So he got his punishment.

The other two are still making trouble in the township. I am still scared of them. I am still scared of what they might do to me, or my sister.

When I got sick with the liver, when I was in hospital ... I started to have dreams. The same dream. Jonathan saying to me, 'Solomon, tell my mother I wasn't scared.' Then Jonathan's face becomes my face, and then the shot wakes me up.

In my culture, the last person to see someone alive is supposed to speak at the funeral. You are supposed to tell the listeners what you saw and what you heard so that the living can be at peace with the whole story, with the truth around the death. If you do not do this, then you can become sick, you can be cursed with bad memories and bad dreams. I think that is why I got so sick.

I've been coming here for years, watching you – trying to find the right time. Carrying this thing with me. Walking with it.

Then last year I went to the mountain, to the initiation school. I became a man. On the mountain we are taught to face our responsibilities or always stay ikwekwe[4]... a boy.

[1] Slap.

[2] Fuck off you queer!

[3] Go away!

[4] A small boy

Notes

DECKY DOES A BRONCO
by Douglas Maxwell

Decky Does a Bronco was first performed at Brodie Park, Paisley on 28 July 2000, before embarking on a Scottish tour. In 2010 Grid Iron remounted the play for a tenth anniversary production which toured in Scotland and England.

Broncoing (kicking the swing over the bar) is a dangerous mixture of vandalism and sport. Decky is one of the friends who can't Bronco and tragedy ensues. Chrissy, who is described as a fiery fighter of a boy, bitterly recalls how he felt when his best friend Decky got killed.

CHRISSY – LATE TEENS (SCOTTISH)

Everyone's going nuts. You should see his house. Everyone dies sometime. He was hanging about up at the swings all night, what did you expect?

Look I know it's sad an' that but you'd be better just getting over it. It's not like you were his brother or anything. It's all right to cry and all of that if you're in his family but there's no point if you just hung about with him.

And if he *was* here we'd still be taking the mickey out of him. Just 'cause he's – just 'cause he's no here people are going to be all 'Aw wee Decky was ace man, I was best pals with him' but they werenae. I'm no even going to the funeral.

See aw the folk in his house, they were just as bad. They were loving it. They were pretending to be sad, but you could tell that they were enjoying it. Probably the most interesting thing that's happened to them in their whole lives. They never even knew Decky but they're straight round his house greetin'. I hate people. Well I'm not doing it. I'm not joining in on it 'cause it's not real.

Ach, who cares. Half the stuff they're saying isnae true anyway. Probably. They said he was found in the Bank Burn.

They said the guy had pulled his pants down.

So. No one's going on these swings.

I said no one's going on these swings! These swings are finished. No one's going to Bronco ever again on these swings.

Notes

TOO FAST

by Douglas Maxwell

Too Fast *was originally produced as part of National Theatre Connections 2011. The play is an ensemble comedy for young performers with a strong emotional heart and a huge theatrical reveal in the final scene.*

Spoke's brother has just given a reading in church at the funeral of his friend who died in a car crash.

This speech doesn't have to be done with a Scottish accent.

SPOKE'S BROTHER – 13/14 (SCOTTISH)

What the hell am I doing back in here? I was supposed to go and sit with my mum and dad! Sake. Oh well. Would you all like to know how it went? Would it be useful if I describe, in detail, my recent experiences? To give you, you know, an idea of what awaits you on the other side?

Yeah it went okay actually. Nervous though see. *(His hands are shaking.)* **I was all right until I looked up. They're even standing outside, all the way up the gravel to the graveyard. And there's speakers out there so everyone can hear. But a stand must've broken or something because Mr Gibbons is up on a plastic chair, holding a speaker in both hands, like this. I thought, god, whatever I say next will vibrate in his arms. It'll go all the way back to the graves. And when I looked back down at the reading I couldn't make out the words anymore. I could see them, but as like, marks on paper, not as real words with meanings. I heard someone say 'poor kid'. But I wasn't upset. Well, not until then. Cos then, after that, the meanings kind of came into focus. And now it *did* seem sad. Sad that all these words – every word from now on in – will vibrate nowhere near Ali. And I thought 'Poor Kid'. But I just read it. Without thinking or feeling or meaning or anything. And got off. I concentrated on not tripping and anyway ... it went okay.**

Notes

VELOCITY
by Daniel MacDonald

Velocity was first performed at Persephone Theatre, Saskatoon, SK, Canada on 16 February 2011. Its European premiere was at the Finborough Theatre on 27 April 2014.

The play is about a precocious 15-year-old girl, Dot. Tired with her parents' laid-back attitude to her upbringing, she wants to shake things up and change the family dynamics. So, she decides to explode her father out of the 73rd floor of his office building – just like a science experiment – and as he falls, she interviews him and her mother.

Here, we see Jee, one of Dot's friends, and his friend Ming dancing with Dot's dad – while dancing Jee starts to open up, or at least that's what we think …

JEE – 18/20 (SOUTH ASIAN/MIDDLE EASTERN)

God, white people think they know everything.

My grandparents grew up in post-colonial butt-swamp. In a village the size of my brown thumb with borrowed land from a man who demanded my mom's niece as partial payment to be allowed to suck a few dirty potatoes out of some sad, yellow soil. Name something, bitch. For being confused for an Arab Muslim so often that I decide to pretend to be one of them just to fuck people up. Like the 80 people on the bus who cringe up at me while I playfully fiddle with my backpack. Name something. The fact that I have more in common with white boy Jason, the football quarterback from the suburbs doesn't seem to matter to the cop on the subway who stares at me sideways and is ready to shoot me in the face if I so much as trip over my feet. Like what the fuck is up with the colour of THIS! *(He pulls on a piece of his skin from his cheek and holds it.)* Cause, you know what? My friends don't give a shit! No one I know and love gives a shit. So why do you? Why does the world give a fuckin shit?? Bitch, for being descended from a place so pathetic that people move into the city with the zealous knowledge that whoring your children out is a lucrative option, a step up. And you know what, Mr. D? The wonder of it all is that there's always someone to blame. I can be absolved for hitting my kids, gang raping the villagers,

Notes

shooting every boy over 13, launching a rocket from Heaven and destroying a neighbourhood to kill ONE FUCKIN GUY! ... no matter how stupid I get, there's always someone bigger, better, higher, stupider than me I can blame. And you keep blaming the next guy and the next guy and the next until we find you. Up here on the 73rd floor. 'Cause there's not much above this, right? I mean above this is like ... God, right? And who's gonna blame fucking God? That's the beauty about God. That's why God's so perfect. He's always on your side. DO YOU GET IT MR. D? THAT'S WHY I'M SO FUCKING ANGRY!

I'm just kiddin, man. I don't give a shit. I live in Cedar View Meadows Estates. We got gates and everything. My parents own, like four strip malls.

Notes

FEAR OF MUSIC

(FROM THE COLLECTION *WHAT YOU WISH FOR IN YOUTH*)
by Barney Norris

Fear of Music *was first presented by Up In Arms in association with
Out of Joint at York Theatre Royal on 19 February 2013.*

*The play is a two-hander dealing with the complex relationship
between two brothers, Luke and Andy, spanning from 1988 to 1993
and set in their house in Andover. Their father is dead and their
mother's mental health is fast declining. Luke has recently returned
from university. Andy is into rock music and has ambitions to join
the army, like his dad.*

*Here, older brother Luke is recording the top forty while speculating
whether or not a bird that flew into their window earlier, had died.
Andy then reveals that he once killed a badger.*

ANDY – 15 (UK)

I killed a badger once. I was cycling, and I'd just written this
really wicked song. It was really wicked. Like, really wicked.
And I was freewheeling down this hill singing the chorus, you
know, to get the chorus right, and because it was really wicked,
and these three badgers ran out in front of me. I hit the first
two on the nose and missed the third one. Didn't come off my
bike, I was like, waay, like – wobbling and braking. Second
badger I hit got up and ran off. But the first one, I'd broken
its neck. It was thrashing its arse on the road like this. *(He
mimes a badger with a broken neck dying.)* I went back to it, and
I picked up a stick, because you're meant to finish them off.
But like, badgers are well hard and theirs jaws lock when they
bite, so I couldn't stamp on it or anything, so I got a stick. And
by the time I got back to it, it had stopped thrashing, it was
just breathing really heavily. I stood over it, and watched it
breathe, and then it took this really big breath and I thought,
that's its last breath. And it was either like it was trying to get
enough to keep living. Or like it was saying goodbye. And then
its eyes went blank. I got it off the road with the stick and next
time I went past someone had moved it.

Notes

WISE GUYS
by Philip Osment

First produced at Theatre Centre and Red Ladder Company 1997.

Three young guys living on the edge of society are trying to survive in a fractured world; out of frustration, they turn to crime and drugs.

At the opening of the play, Mike describes how awful it is to live with his drunken abusive father.

MIKE – LATE TEENS (UK)

So that bastard comes home drunk again. Front door slams. Falls over my brother Martin's bike in the hall doesn't he?

I can hear him coming up the stairs. Freddy Krueger. Knocking the picture off the wall. Gave it to my Mum for her birthday. Can hear the glass splinter.

I look over at Martin. He's just lying there. His eyes open. Got the look my hamster used to get when the cat came in the room.

And then his fist smashes into my face. And I'm on the floor and he's laying into me. And she's trying to stop him but he sends her flying along the landing and she bashes her head against the toilet door. He's got the end of the hoover and he's beating me over the head with it.

And then it's over. He's out the door. And she's running after him trying to stop him. Stupid cow. She's running down the street and all the neighbours are watching. Blood dripping off her chin down her night-dress. What a sight. She wants him to stay. Couldn't give a toss about me.

My brother Martin looks like one of those kids you see on TV at Christmas singing carols. Angelic. He's not. But he looks like it. I always felt like I had to protect him. 'Cos he was so much younger. I've been mean to him, don't get me wrong. Stole my Walkman and broke it one time. Closest I ever came to losing it with him. I mean I thumped him but not like to really hurt him. I'd never do that. At the end of the day he's the only person I care about. And I'm the only person he cares about. My Mum says I got too much influence over him. She's scared I'm going to lead him astray. I nearly got done for nicking car stereos and she's scared I'll get him into that. But I wouldn't. I'd kill him if he started that.

Notes

THE SAINTS
by Luke Barnes

The Saints was first performed on 5 August 2014 as part of the Art at the Heart festival at Nuffield Playing Field in Guildhall Square, Southampton. Nuffield Playing Field was built by Assemble Architects. The festival was supported by The Sackler Foundation, Arts Council England and Southampton City Council.

Kenny Glynn is the world's biggest Saints fan. He is infatuated with Emily and is desperate to take her out. She is bemused by his forthright approach and keeps rejecting him because he's a bit too weird for her liking but he's very persistent and won't take no for an answer.

KENNY – TEENS (UK)

I like your hair.

I like your nose as well.

I drank a whole pint of milk and threw up on the floor yesterday.

I er ... I ...

I love you. I'm gonna be a footballer one day and I'm gonna need a WAG. Can we get married and have babies and one day I can take you on a holiday to France and we can sit in a tent and kiss all day and share a toothbrush and have sex?

Let's start.

(To audience or to himself.)

There is no worse combination than standing at a party with your trousers down, thirty kids and a clown laughing at your willy and your mum walking in to tell you your father's died.

Nothing will ever go worse than this.

(Back to the girl.)

I've been thinking about you giving me the party bag, it was really nice. I've been thinking about it loads and now Dad's dead I just thought I should say all the things I want to in case I never get to say them. I wanted to say thank you and wanted to ask you ...

Notes

I feel really embarrassed about it. What's the matter? Are you going through menopause? My mum gets that. I understand it –

I was just ... I was just wondering if you wanted to come to mine tomorrow after school and play FIFA?

How about Tuesday?

How about Wednesday? People don't do much on Wednesdays so it might be nice to relax.

You do something the first three nights of the week?

OK great. Well I'll knock next weekend. See ya then.

I'll save you a place in assembly.

Lunch then. See ya then.

Great I'll meet you at the gates after school.

I just want to hang out with you.

Maybe some other time?*

YES! SOME OTHER TIME!

She wants to see me another time! GET IN!

(To audience or to himself.) If you don't keep shooting, you'll never score a goal. One day Emily will be my girlfriend and from this point on – Emily is my FA Cup and I am Southampton.

This line is spoken by Emily in the playtext. Here, I suggest including it as part of Kenny's monologue.

Notes

20s

LUNGS
by Duncan Macmillan

Lungs *opened in Washington DC in autumn 2011 followed by a Paines Plough and Sheffield Crucible production in October 2011.*

The play is a two-hander. A couple are deciding their future. They're educated and considered, they want to have a child for the right reasons. But living in the midst of political unrest, and acutely aware of environmental concerns, their relationship is tested.

Here, the couple are in bed; they've been musing about the news of their forthcoming baby. 'M' then opens up about life, death and his feelings.

M – LATE 20s/30s (UK)

I've always thought

I'm okay, I'm an okay person. A normal enough person. Basically, you know, good.

,

I wish I'd read more when I was younger. Or just, maybe slept with more people. Or travelled. It's going to be harder to travel now you know, with

,

nothing's ending. It's the start of something. I'm young. We're young. It's exciting.

Can't tell if my eyes are open. Am I keeping you awake?

Just can't stop thinking. Everything. Life. The universe.

Death.

Try to picture what I'll look like. Dead. Stopped. Just another object in the room. Who'll see me like that. What my expression will be. When the face just relaxes it looks sort of sarcastic I think. My dead face.

If it's going to happen, the solution to it all, the survival of mankind, it will happen in our lifetime. It has to. And we'll be alive to witness it.

When we're talking I can't take my eyes off you. You're so honest with me and it hurts sometimes but I remind myself

Notes

you only say these things because you trust me. That I'm an anchor or something, I'm a nucleus to your proton, is that right? I think sometimes you think we're having a conversation and that I'm listening and responding but really I'm only silent because I have no idea what to say. You're like an animal, a hungry, wild animal and you're circling me and snarling and you're beautiful and exciting and you're trusting me because I'm standing still but really I'm just frozen to the spot, really I just don't know what else to do and I worry that sometimes you think that that's strength and it's not, it's not, it's just

I dreamt that the baby had been born but it was just a cloud. A little thunder cloud. Or a squirming little creature with fangs and claws and flashing eyes.

I'll take a book off the shelf, any book and you'll have turned down the pages and underlined things. Put stars in the margins. And I stare at the sentence you've highlighted. I'll reread the paragraph. I'll think what has she seen that I can't see? What is it that I don't understand?

Notes

LUNGS
by Duncan Macmillan

Lungs opened in Washington DC in autumn 2011 followed by a Paines Plough and Sheffield Crucible production in October 2011.

The play is a two-hander. A couple are deciding their future. They're educated and considered, they want to have a child for the right reasons. But living in the midst of political unrest, and acutely aware of environmental concerns, their relationship is tested.

This speech comes at the very end of the play; after having split up for a while, they are now both willing to give their relationship a second chance.

M – LATE 20s/30s (UK)

It's not the perfect circumstances, but let's go into this with open arms. I love you. Okay? I always have. When I'm away from you I forget how to enjoy anything and when I'm with you I feel at home.

We've never worked out how to be together without making each other feel a bit shit and I want to find a way to not do that. You've got to stop ripping bits off me and I've got to grow up and behave like an actual human being.

You've needed me to know what you need without having to ask. You've needed me to be aware of how I'm feeling and to let you in to my head. Right now I know exactly what you need to hear and it's absolutely what I'm feeling.

We're not going to overthink this.

We're doing this.

We're going to get the books and go to classes and work out how to be parents. And we're going to grow old together and look back on all this and laugh because it will seem like a different lifetime.

And we'll have a conversation and we'll just try to do the right thing. Because we're good people. Right?

And we'll plant forests. I mean it. We'll cycle everywhere. We'll grow our own food if we have to. We'll never take another plane. We'll just stay right here. And we'll plant forests.

Notes

CARTHAGE
by Chris Thompson

First performed at the Finborough Theatre as a staged reading as part of Vibrant 2012 – A Festival of Finborough Playwrights *in 2012. The first full production of* Carthage *opened at the Finborough Theatre on 28 January 2014.*

Tommy Anderson was born in a prison, and he died in one too. His mother Anne, blames Marcus, the prison officer who was supposed to be looking after him. Marcus was acquitted by the courts but remains tormented by his role in Tommy's death; he appeals to Anne for forgiveness.

MARCUS – LATE 20s (UK)

Please, listen to me.

You say you want me to ask forgiveness from you and –

I need you to forgive me. I do need that.

But I was found not guilty, Anne, and what I'm saying is that if you could accept that, then we maybe could come together and talk. It's good that you asked me here, I should have come sooner, you're right, but we should talk about this and I don't know, some day, you know at some point, you might forgive me for my involvement but understand at the same time that I wasn't responsible.

Because I know I was involved, I'm not saying I wasn't. I'm saying that I was found not guilty but I know I should be – well, I want to be – I mean, given what happened, it's quite right that I should come to you and –

I was so nervous coming here today. I've tried before. Fucking so many times, I get off the bus, but I can't get myself through the gates. I've been stood outside for two hours today, but I made myself come in. I was determined today. I was so nervous, but I was determined to do it, Anne. I have to explain what I said in court – I never meant to say it was his own fault, I'd never say that about a child, that isn't what I meant, but they learn the system these kids do, Anne, and it's hard on them, because sometimes they do just want a hug, as lame as that sounds – but they don't get hugs in places like prisons.

Notes

It's not my job to go around giving hugs out, I kind of assume that's someone else's job, but they still crave that intimacy though – they crave being held, don't they? I'm sure they do. And I can see how you might think that came across as me blaming Tommy, I totally see that, but what I was trying to say was that sometimes kids engineer these situations that they know will result in restraint because what they really want is to be held and cuddled – contained, I guess, and that's what I meant when I said –

Sorry, I was so nervous coming here today.

MARCUS *may be crying.*

Forgive me. Please forgive me.

Notes

PINEAPPLE
by Phillip McMahon

Pineapple *premiered at the Droichead Arts Centre on 29 April 2011 in a production by Calipo Theatre Company in association with the Drogheda Arts Festival.*

A play about Paula, her teenage sister Roxanna, and a group of friends – four women and one man – set in the Ballymun Flats. It explores family, love and friendship. Dan has just met the women, but he finds himself in the flat drinking Smirnoff Ice, getting tipsy but not drunk. Dan gets teased about why he's so dressed up.

This speech doesn't have to be done with an Irish accent.

DAN – 28/30 (IRISH)

I was out with a girl, wasn't I?

Don't look so surprised.

It was going okay. I was being funny, *(to ANTOINETTE)* shut up! She was havin' a good time I reckon. It was a blind date yoke – through a mate at work – one of those … but yeah, we were havin' fun. I took her for dinner – you know, nothin' fancy or anything, just a place at the back of a pub and I had the – I dunno – some sort of skewer thing and she had a prawn cocktail thing to start and then she went on to have a Sea Bass and I was thinkin', you know – that's a lot of fish – but she *had* said something about being a part-time vegetarian, so maybe she only eats seafood. Anyway it comes to like – just before the bill comes and she – now just before I tell you, I actually don't care right – but she farts at the table/

/and I laughed, 'cos I thought it was funny, or cute – I didn't care basically – we all do it. But she leapt up out of her seat and legged it to the jacks – and I'm sat there not knowin' whether I should pay the bill or what, because I know *your* crowd can be quite sensitive about that, so I waited …

Well she comes back and says that she's sick – like dodgy food or something, and I'm all up for complaining to the kitchen or the waiter or whoever but she's – Grainne's her name – she just says that it's best to be at home if she's not well … then I say that maybe she just needs to sit on the jacks for a bit.

20s
86/87

Notes

You know, like, trying to be sound – but she was like a rocket then; out the door – no mention of the bill or anything ...

Ah – I wasn't that into it anyways. I've got trust issues with vegetarians. Part-time or otherwise.

Fuck it I suppose. You win some, you lose some.

Notes

PINEAPPLE
by Phillip McMahon

Pineapple *premiered at the Droichead Arts Centre on 29 April 2011 in a production by Calipo Theatre Company in association with the Drogheda Arts Festival.*

A play about Paula, her teenage sister Roxanna, and a group of friends – four women and one man – set in the Ballymun Flats. It explores family, love and friendship. In this speech Dan is opening up to love interest Paula who has just asked him 'Well if you're not married, what's wrong with ya?'

This speech doesn't have to be done with an Irish accent.

DAN – 28/30 (IRISH)

I bottled it.

I didn't rock up at the church.

It's true. School mates, friends, work people ... they were all there, hats at the ready ... my family, her family ... But I just couldn't ... I had this knot in my stomach that was just saying, *No.*

She was a lovely girl, but she didn't make me feel anything but ordinary, you know? I'm not looking for fireworks every time I look at someone, but I do want to feel ... something. I want to be excited.

Not in that way! Well actually, yes, in that way too ... but in loads of ways ...

I'm not proud of it. But an hour later and we'd have spent our lives miserable or trying to get out of it.

She sent me an email. She hasn't spoken to me since – but she actually said thanks and went on to list the reasons why we shouldn't be together – and she was petty enough at times but she spoke loads of sense too – like she was more straight-talking and sensible in those few lines than she had been in eight years of going out, so I was like – *good for you* – and at the end of the mail she wrote in CAPS the main reason she was glad we didn't get married ...

Because *she* didn't love me.

Notes

And I was like – *snap* – and *good* – because it means that we did the right thing. And it made me wonder then why I asked her and why she said yes – but then we do that kind of thing all the time because it's easier, isn't it – than being on your own?

Am I talkin' too much?

Notes

PERFECT MATCH
by Gary Owen

The play premiered as part of the Ideal World Season at Watford Palace Theatre.

The play is a comedy and the premise poses a pertinent question; whether it's possible to find our perfect partner, or whether we're better off leaving it to chance.

Aaron was going out with Lorna for six years but then through online dating he found his perfect match in Anna. Here, he is trying to level and reason with Lorna to get her blessing for not just his newfound relationship with Anna, but also their impending wedding.

AARON – 20s (UK)

She's just ... incredibly sweet.

What I don't like is, people pretending to be sweet,
And then throwing a strop when they don't get their way.
But when the sweetness isn't pretend
When it comes from a really real place ... I love that.
Like the reason I'm here tonight is
Cos she feels bad about you. Cos she's so sweet.

She hates the idea of us marrying
And it being like a horrible thing for you.
She says it will basically ruin the day for her
If we marry, without your blessing.

She just cares. She cares about you.
And who are you?
I mean as far as she's concerned.

Lorna ...

Listen: you know, when you sit like this.

AARON sits, one foot on the other knee.

And you spot there's some mud, dried up, in the tread of your shoe. And you're going to dig it out with your finger. But then – it might not be mud. It might be dog crap. And actually, digging dog crap out of your shoe, that's nasty. That's horrible. So maybe ... if it's all dried up, if it doesn't smell, maybe you just leave it. You walk round with crap on your shoe, for months. And that, is how I've treated you.

Notes

Like dried-up dog crap, on the bottom of my shoe. *(Beat.)* You deserved far better.

You should hate my guts. You have every right.

So I'm going to sit here with you, cos I promised Anna I would,
Take everything you've got to throw at me.
And then I'm going to go, and meet her,
And she'll say, 'How's poor Lorna taking it?'

I'll say, 'Well it's been really hard, for Lorna.

'But she's being really brave.
'She just wants me, to be really really happy.
'Darling: we have her blessing.'

I now exist solely to meet Anna's needs.
She needs to live in a world where you don't hate us?
I will make that world her reality.

Notes

INNOCENCE
by Dea Loher
Translated by David Tushingham

This translation of Innocence *was commissioned by the Goethe Institut and was first produced in the UK by the Arcola Theatre in association with KP Productions on 6 January 2010.*

Innocence *takes place in a city by the sea. It's about fourteen people on the edge. A darkly comic panorama of urban restlessness.*

Fadoul is an illegal immigrant keen to avoid any contact with the police. As a result, he has dissuaded his friend Elisio from rescuing a drowning woman. Fadoul has just found a large sum of money in a carrier bag at a bus stop.

FADOUL – 20s (BLACK/AFRICAN)

My hiding place for the money is behind one of the asbestos sheets and my mouth is – sewn shut. My first thought, forgery. How do 200,089 euros 77 cents end up under a bench in a bus stop. Two-hun-dred-thou-sand euros. In used notes. Plus eighty-nine euros seventy-seven cents in coins. So I take one of the 50-euro-notes – four thousand 50-euro-notes – and buy cigarettes in a supermarket where they have one of those machines. I tell the assistant, look at me, I'm black as the varnish on a piano and look at this note, a 50-euro-note, in your position I would put this note under your lamp as fast as possible because it's probably not genuine. She refuses, she says she's not a racist, she looks at me and says she trusts me. Why. It's not a question of trust, I tell her, it's a question of experience. Or not. She says, she doesn't understand why I want to provoke her she's got nothing against foreigners. Good, I say, great, I say, now please do your duty and test whether this note is genuine; there are rules, aren't there, that every 50-euro-note has to be tested for its genuineness or is there a special bonus for black people, do I get preferential treatment because I'm black or something. She said, to see if it's genuine, there's no such word as genuineness, and she would have tested the note herself ages ago if I hadn't said such stupid things to her right from the start, because she doesn't let people say stupid things to her, not even black people. I, confused by this white dialectic, say why has she been specially nice to me although I get on her nerves;

Notes

if someone gets on my nerves, I am deliberately not nice to them, and she says yes, that's exactly what you're trying to achieve, you want me to lose my temper because I've been provoked, I say, why would I provoke you, I just want to know if she knows whether this note is genuine or not and I want to know too so that we can all sleep peacefully again and she says, in a challenging way, then go to a bank and you'll find out and I say I've just come from a bank, I've just been to the bank, but I don't trust them and she looks at me and says, stupid arsehole and puts the note under her lamp and says, it's genuine and I say, thanks love, thought so.

I'm a simple person. I don't understand anything about – politics. Or science. But I was brave enough to run away. What I know I've left behind me.

And all this, me, what I am, who I am and how I am, my entire life, is dependent on a single letter. My life, my fate are dependent on this single letter: A-m-erican A-f-rican.

There you have my life in two words.

I'll tell you what I believe.

God is in this bag.

And there's no proof of God except ourselves.

Notes

EVENTIDE
by Barney Norris

Eventide was first presented by Up In Arms and Arcola Theatre in association with the North Wall on 25 September 2015.

The play is set in a rural village pub in Hampshire. There's only three characters, the publican, his young friend Mark and the village organist. They have very different lives but are bonded by a sense of dissatisfaction.

Here, we see Mark open up for the first time about the loss of a girl he grew up with; he finally admits that he loved her.

MARK – 20's (UK)

It's strange. Cos I did care for her, I can admit that now, I did. Yeah. And I feel – but I've no more right to grieve than anyone else, have I. Cos. No reason to feel any – more than anyone else. We were close for a while, at school or whatever, yeah, and I loved all that, when we were at school, but not for any real reason, only because we shared a few classes, you know? And I've never had the kind of girlfriend where you're – you know, where you're happy, so I don't know, but I think people who are close like, I mean properly close, like, maybe I mean people who are in love, sort of thing, there must always be more to it than that, mustn't there? Some – feeling you both have, which is more than just sharing a few classes, and you fancying her and her not minding you. Which is more or less. Maybe not for the likes of me, maybe I'll end up taking what I can get or have to stay on my own forever, or whatever, but for the likes of her, you know? There must be actual love that's like a thing, that exists. So I don't feel more important than anyone else. No. I don't feel I should be, anyway. So it's strange how I'm feeling today.

Notes

OPERATION CRUCIBLE
by Kieran Knowles

The play was first performed at the Finborough Theatre on 1 December 2013.

Inspired by real events, the play takes place on and around 12 December 1940 – the day of the Sheffield Blitz ('Operation Crucible' was the German code name for the attack).

At 11.44 p.m. on the night of the raid, a single 500kg bomb reduced the Marples Hotel, which stood proudly in Fitzalan Square, from seven storeys to just fifteen feet of rubble. Only one of the ten compartments in the hotel's cellars withstood the blast. Within it, trapped, were four men.

Here, the men are sharing stories with each other.

ARTHUR – 27 (UK)

We had time. That were the weird thing. Normally danger is something immediate. But while we waited we were stuck in suspended time. Waiting for rescue – or waiting to die.

I'd used me belt to tie around me leg, slow the blood you know. And I'd torn a piece of me shirt, cleanest bit I could find and put it on the cut. Been holding it there for hours. Covered in blood. Simple stuff really. Things you learn in the Mill. This were a bad one but I'd seen much worse.

It were good training. Working in factory, prepared you for the front line, when the war came to you. Because it teaches you not to panic. You may lose a finger, bang your head, burn yourself but if you stay calm, keep your head in the right place, you'll get through it.

In here! Down here! We're here!

We shouted.

Nothing.

Please! Please.

Please.

Scuffling. Shuffling. Miles above.

Notes

Voices. We heard voices.

Here! We're here!

It felt like we'd been down here for hours.

We could hear them.

Pulling away the fallen bricks.

Closer. Nearer. Just above. Then -

I'm out, finally I'm out.

I'm running and I see smoke rising over't city.

The light's blinding but it's not bright just grey. The weather isn't. It isn't this it isn't that, it just isn't. Nothing, just grey bit foggy that's it.

I feel my feet skimming over the debris on the road, I can hear the deep scratching sound as my shoes catch and drag slightly, only very short but unmistakeable. My leg is screaming with pain. I hear engine noise and people talking, chattering, crying – I hear but I'm not listening, I'm not there.

I hear someone shout at me, a woman, dirt all over her face, she comes screaming to me and pointing in alarm. I follow her finger, follow her gaze.

Smoke curls from three streets away and the wind blows it all the way till it's hovering just above my head. I reach up and run my hands through it. It's thick. It's leading me home.

I'm twenty-seven.

And me Dad must have been forty-six/forty-seven.

He'd been under't table. A bomb landed just a few yards from front door, it demolished the place. The whole thing came down. His hands were limp, grazed, lifeless.

I move towards him, with each step I feel the whole weight of me body.

I kneel beside him. Lay me hand on his chest.

It's still.

All the power he had, all the confidence and ... gone. He looks peaceful, like he's sleeping.

I run me hand through his greying hair. Tuck it behind his ears. I lean over, kiss him on forehead, like he used to do to me.

Notes

'It's never been worse than this, Dad ... Never.'

I stood. Stepped back. Took one last look and then turned and walked away.

I kept walking.

Notes

CHAPEL STREET
by Luke Barnes

Chapel Street *was first produced by Scrawl for the Edinburgh Festival as part of the Old Vic New Voices Edinburgh Season 2012 in partnership with the Underbelly and supported by IdeasTap.*

The play is a lively two-hander. It's Friday night and we follow Joe and Kirsty in their separate worlds, narrate and document their evening, until the two finally meet on Chapel Street.

Here, Joe is out on the town ready to have the night of his life.

In the play the characters speak to the audience but you can invent the person you are talking to.

JOE – 23 (UK)

Last time we were out it was magic. It was one of those days were it's like three o'clock and you just know that the whole day lies in front you? You can taste the air. It's palpable. It's real. And the future is like in your hand. I was sitting in the beer garden of that pub next to the train station with Jonno and Woggy, same as every Friday, but this Friday was special. Because tomorrow. Tomorrow Woggy was leaving. Tomorrow Woggy was getting on a train and he might never come back.

Parked in the corner was a white van right and some angry-looking fucker sitting in the front seat. He'd just had a proper little scuffle with the landlord, been kicked out and was burning up in his car. Sort of like when you trap a bee inside a glass and watch it twat its own head on the side of the glass. Before I knew what was going on he'd got out and stormed towards us. I pretended my phone rang and walked away. He stormed past and back into the pub. Obviously like being a nosy cunt I followed him in to hear what was going on and do you know what he said right? Get this. He goes 'Listen you fat cunt, if you don't serve me now, I'm gonna go out to the car, get a shotgun and shoot you in the face.' Somebody must have overheard right because next thing I know I'm back in the garden and the pigs are all there round this white van. They open it up. And guess what they find? Shotgun, loaded. They took him off in the car and no one saw him again. All the time there were dirty little kids watching from the wall. Muddy Hands. Weird how I remember that.

Notes

It's funny to think that like the person we were pissing ourselves at was actually carrying a shotgun like in the back of his car.

We could have seen Tony the barman get a bullet in his face. What the fuck?! That's like mental. If that had kicked off it could have been us caught in the crossfire and for a second I got this image of my mother walking behind my coffin at my funeral. And she looked so sad. Then I started thinking like, fuck, if I died tomorrow I would have died having done nothing. So I made a promise there and then to Jonno and Woggy that tonight we would live tonight like it was our last, for all we know we might never see Woggy again. 'You're going to have that all the fucking time as of next week Wogster.' And with that I bought a round.

Notes

CHAPEL STREET
by Luke Barnes

Chapel Street *was first produced by Scrawl for the Edinburgh Festival as part of the Old Vic New Voices Edinburgh Season 2012 in partnership with the Underbelly and supported by IdeasTap.*

The play is a lively two-hander. It's Friday night and we follow Joe and Kirsty in their separate worlds, narrate and document their evening, until the two finally meet on Chapel Street.

Here, Joe is out on the town ready to have the night of his life.

In the play the characters speak to the audience but you can invent the person you are talking to.

JOE – 23 (UK)

Two beautiful girls drive past in an open-top Mercedes. Dealer's girls no doubt. And they look at us and make a sick face, yano like a *(Sick face.)* ... So I toast to them crashing the fucker, arrogant tarts.

So by five right, I am fucking steaming. Like proper steaming. Then Cassie walks in. She looks fucking good. She had the tits. She had the legs. She had fucking everything down to the Kurt whatshisface shoes so I sit there like speechless yano cause I literally haven't seen her for years except on Facebook and here she is standing right in front of me looking fit, with her black hair looking all black and her deep brown eyes looking awesome.

And here am I off my tits at five o'clock dressed like fucking Bob the Builder. You see the way it works: you spend all your time, sitting in the same pub, on the same day of the week, looking at the same girls and then when you get the one you want they get away. 'Alright darling,' I say real smoothly like.

She walks straight past me doesn't even say hello. Fucking good. Stupid bitch.

I notice her looking over we catch eyes and I give her like a matey smile yano, the type that mates do but because I'm fucked it looks like I'm taking the piss, something like this. *(Face.)* Fuck I'm a cunt. She gives me one of those 'Why the fuck did I ever waste my time with some little gimp like you'

20s

Notes

faces and like thrusts herself around, yano when people like try to prove a point that they're pissed off about something. *(Shows.)*

This is like God telling me by every means possible that I should get unbelievably smashed and have like the best night ever. I'm shit at this game, so I'm necking fingers everywhere.

Notes

CHAPEL STREET
by Luke Barnes

Chapel Street *was first produced by Scrawl for the Edinburgh Festival as part of the Old Vic New Voices Edinburgh Season 2012 in partnership with the Underbelly and supported by IdeasTap.*

The play is a lively two-hander. It's Friday night and we follow Joe and Kirsty in their separate worlds, narrate and document their evening, until the two finally meet on Chapel Street.

Here, Joe returns home from his night on the lash.

In the play the characters speak to the audience but you can invent the person you are talking to.

JOE – 23 (UK)

I walk home and when I get in Mum gives me all this shit. I'm like 'Please just go to sleep Mum, I've just shat more ale than you've drank in the last 20 years so can you just fuck off.' I whack a cheeky one off before I go to sleep. And in the morning I go the shops to get a massive bottle of Coke and ready salted crisps. Some kids asked me to get served. Fuck it. I go into the shop, ask the Pakistan ... Uzbekistani, whatever he is for a half bottle of vodka and I give it them. May as well give them something to make the moment worth living eh. They look fucking bored. I know what it's like to be bored. I'm bored. I want a job that's not boring. All the jobs here are so shit they're just fucking serving people. Wearing shit hats. I know people need to do these jobs and if they stopped the whole world would. I know that, I'm not dissing it. But no one gives a fuck about them. They're battery hens. Fuck that. I deserve better than that. I want to DO something. I want a job so I can sit down in a club and buy a girl a drink and not give a fuck. There you are darling. Have one on me.

I had to borrow 20 quid off me mum to go out tonight.

I know it's my fault. I know that if I tried I could work, get fit, get a girlfriend, get a job, take up footy again and my life would change completely. But that's all a bit scary isn't it.

I'm not going to do anything with my life am I.

Might as well get fucked.

Notes

The world is the ride of life, and I'm on the front row with a big fucking bag of popcorn. Laughing away with my mates and smiling. We can't change the tracks we just have to sit and go. Enjoy the view and laugh on the way.

But for now it's time to go out.

At least we've got this to look forward to.

From the cradle to the casket, Friday night will always be good.

That's what it's there for. And this one will be good. This one will be really fucking good.

Notes

RED

by John Logan

Red was first performed at Donmar Warehouse, London on 3 December 2009.

The play is a two-hander, set in New York City, circa 1958-1959. Mark Rothko is a real-life famous American painter. Ken is an aspiring painter and his newly appointed assistant. Rothko has a fierce reputation; after being his student, gofer, scapegoat, Ken finally dares to speak up and challenge him.

KEN – 20s (USA)

Do you know where I live in the city?

Uptown? Downtown? Brooklyn?

You know if I'm married? Dating? Queer? Anything?

Two years I've been working here. Eight hours a day, five days a week and you know nothing about me. You ever once asked me to dinner? Maybe come to your house?

You know I'm a painter, don't you?

Have you ever once asked to look at my work?

Christ almighty, try working for *you* for a living! – The talking-talking-talking-jesus-christ-won't-he-ever-shut-up titanic self-absorption of the man! You stand there trying to look so deep when you're nothing but a solipsistic bully with your grandiose self-importance and lectures and arias and let's-look-at-the-fucking-canvas-for-another-few-weeks-let's-not-fucking-paint-let's-just-look. And the *pretension*! Jesus Christ, the *pretension*! I can't imagine any other painter in the history of art ever tried so hard to be SIGNIFICANT!

Not everything has to be so goddamn IMPORTANT all the time! Not every painting has to rip your guts out and expose your soul! Not everyone wants art that actually HURTS! Sometimes you just want a fucking still life or landscape or soup can or comic book! Which you might learn if you ever actually left your goddamn hermetically sealed *submarine* here with all the windows closed and no natural light – BECAUSE NATURAL LIGHT ISN'T GOOD ENOUGH FOR YOU!

Notes

But then *nothing* is ever good enough for you! Not even the people who buy your pictures! Museums are nothing but mausoleums, galleries are run by pimps and swindlers, and art collectors are nothing but shallow social-climbers. So who *is* good enough to own your art?! Anyone?!

Or maybe the real question is: who's good enough to even *see* your art?... Is it just possible *no one* is worthy to look at your paintings? ... That's it, isn't it?... We have all been 'weighed in the balance and have been found wanting.'

You say you spend your life in search of real 'human beings,' people who can look at your pictures with compassion. But in your heart you no longer believe those people exist ... So you lose faith ... So you lose hope ... So black swallows red.

My friend, I don't think you'd recognize a real human being if he were standing right in front of you.

Notes

THE WELL AND BADLY LOVED
by Ben Webb

The Well and Badly Loved *was first performed on 13 March 2012 at Ovalhouse and has since been translated into Spanish and French.*

This collection of short plays is a passionate response to the effect of Clause 28, the amendment to 1988's Local Government Act, which prohibited local authorities and schools from 'promoting' homosexuality (not repealed until 2003). The plays tell the story of a love affair from three different angles.

This speech is taken from the final instalment, The Actor Has Told of His Pain – *the two lovers Tom and Matt meet again and a third character, Jonny, an ex, helps to give shape to the stories they have been telling each other.*

Here, Jonny is opening up to Tom about Matt in order for him to understand where he's coming from.

JONNY – 20s (GAY/UK)

Matt once pissed on me and I know he loved it. It was written all over his face. For me it was a whole surge of feelings filling up our bodies and passing between us. And I'd love to go back to that place again. To be at the point of knowing him better than anyone else, that moment of infinite possibilities, the intensity of us. Matt's with someone else now though and so am I. We've all moved on. We are each other's past. We are both the things that happened and the things that didn't but no longer the things that might. My new boyfriend won't even piss in the same room as me, let alone on me. That's my life.

Matt and I though we were temporary, transitory. Love always is, right? It was wonderful but it wasn't forever, nothing is. And it doesn't even touch your time with him. It should be the last thing on your mind.

What else can I say?

The first boy I fell in love with was Michael. I loved him maybe for a moment and that one moment kept me at his side for nine months. His love was unequal to mine. It meant so much less to him. But it was my first time and I was not prepared.

Notes

I was not prepared. Because, well, who prepares us for love? When a child cries you hold it and I was a child, even then. He used my body in the passing of time. I let him do it because I knew no better. And I wanted him to do it. I wanted to be used. The first time we fall in love Tom, it feels like forever, but it's only the first time, it's only a start. It means everything and nothing.

Sex isn't just the body stuff it's everything before that, it's everything after. Even without touching there can still be sex, even without the other person knowing, and it's no less real. If only I could go back and fuck some sense into the child I was.

Unforgiveable. And yet I forgive.

Notes

THE WELL AND BADLY LOVED
by Ben Webb

The Well and Badly Loved was first performed on 13 March 2012 at Ovalhouse and has since been translated into Spanish and French.

This collection of short plays is a passionate response to the effect of Clause 28, the amendment to 1988's Local Government Act, which prohibited local authorities and schools from 'promoting' homosexuality (not repealed until 2003). The plays tell the story of a love affair from three different angles.

This speech is taken from the final instalment, The Actor Has Told of His Pain *– the two lovers, Tom and Matt, meet again and a third character, Jonny, an ex, helps to give shape to the stories they have been telling each other.*

Here, Tom is talking to Matt about his feelings for him.

TOM – 20s (GAY/UK)

I've spent so long dreaming. Dreaming of you, dreaming of the past. Now I've started to dream of the future. I have this one dream that keeps coming back. Terrifying dream. End of the world, some kind of apocalypse has happened, some trauma, and I'm alone in the ruins of our old flat. In this dream I know something bad is about to happen and I have to choose whether to stay there and defend or to go on the run. And I can't make the decision. And then I wake up. Decision unmade. And I'm never sure for a moment or so what's real anymore. And I go into my living room, turn on the TV, and there is still the BBC. I look out of the window and there is still the Tesco Express. I pick up my phone and there is still 118 118. The bad things have not happened yet. It was only a dream. But it felt, so real.

All my life I've done things I didn't expect to do. Those have been the good things. I don't know what any of this means. I don't know what I want it to mean. I don't know what I want. Can I touch you? No not yet I just want to sit here close to you close enough it's too early to touch again but can I touch you? Your face is one thing, then it's another, I love that.

I've wanted so long to touch you again but I know that if I do it still may be too soon. Or too late. The wrong moment.

Notes

A mistake. Even the small things have become enormous. And I'm not sure I can bear the consequences. But please let me touch you.

I don't know what you're thinking. I don't know how you feel about anything anymore. What do I have to do to unsilence you? Tell me a story, quiet man. Whisper it in my ear. Write it on my body. Bark us like dogs untethered into the night. Speak. Speak. Speak then.

Notes

30s

THE BODY OF AN AMERICAN
by Dan O'Brien

The play had its European premiere at the Gate Theatre on 16 January 2014 in a co-production between the Gate Theare and Royal & Derngate in Northampton.

Mogadishu, 1993. Dan is an American writer who is struggling to finish his play about ghosts. Paul is a Canadian photojournalist who is about to take a picture that will win him the Pulitzer Prize. Both men live worlds apart but a chance encounter over the airwaves sparks a special friendship. This play is a two-hander which sees two actors jump between more than thirty roles in a new form of documentary drama.

Here, Dan shares an experience he had while writing his play.

DAN – 30s (USA)

I was listening to this podcast. Writing
my play about historical ghosts. Packing
up all our things. It was the very end
of August. It was the end of New York
for us. It was the end of something else,
what? our youth? In Princeton. Which is just so
beautiful this time of year. Every time
of year, really. All the trees and leaves. All
the squirrels. All of the privileged children,
including myself, in some ways. I was
sad to leave. It had been a rough few years.
I'd walk around the campus late at night
and feel almost good about myself. Smart.
Of value. And of course I felt guilty
too, to have had this library. These trees
and squirrels. The beautiful young women
to watch. Unlimited laser printing.
While you're off in Iraq, Paul. Or Kabul.
Or Jakarta, that's where you live, Paul, right?
And Jakarta's in Indonesia. Right?
There was this hangar-sized Whole Foods nearby,
lots of Priuses, and bumper stickers
celebrating the date when Bush would leave
office. I'd go running in thunderstorms

Notes

sometimes. I'd sit on the back porch sipping
vodka, cooking meat on a charcoal grill.
Watching swallows swoop out of a twilit
sky into my maple tree. And your voice
got to me. It's your voice:

                This is you speaking, though
it might as well be me.
                I felt you could have been
talking about playwrights. Without any
real risk. You were mad:
I felt like I knew you. Or I was you
in some alternate reality.

And as I'm packing and listening to you
I'm wondering if I feel so moved because
you sound so messed up.

                Or because you scare me. The haunted
often sound like ghosts, in my experience.
You poor man, who are you?

Notes

THE BODY OF AN AMERICAN
by Dan O'Brien

The play had its European premiere at the Gate Theatre on 16 January 2014 in a co-production between the Gate Theare and Royal & Derngate in Northampton.

Mogadishu, 1993. Dan is an American writer who is struggling to finish his play about ghosts. Paul is a Canadian photojournalist who is about to take a picture that will win him the Pulitzer Prize. Both men live worlds apart but a chance encounter over the airwaves sparks a special friendship. This play is a two-hander which sees two actors jump between more than thirty roles in a new form of documentary drama.

Here, Dan opens up about his family.

DAN – 30s (USA)

                        **My family
stopped talking to me, several years ago,
and I have no idea why. That's not true,
I have many ideas but none of them
make sense. I was about to get married
but it wasn't like they didn't approve
of my wife. It had something to do with
the fact that nobody would be coming
from my family because they have no friends.
I mean literally my parents don't have
any friends. They can barely leave the house
and whatever's left of their own families
won't speak to them for reasons I've never
understood. And I'd just written a play
that was the closest I'd come to writing
autobiography. And my brother** `
**was in the hospital again, for God
knows what exactly, depression mostly.
He hadn't spoken to any of us
in years. Which was mostly okay with me
cause like everyone else in my family
I suppose I just wanted to forget
he'd ever existed at all. Maybe**

30s
140/141

Notes

this was all because of him? reminding
my family of what happened years ago
when I was 12 and he was 17,
one Tuesday afternoon in February
walking up the driveway when I noticed
him coming around the house with his back
all pressed with snow, the back of his head white
with snow, and I thought it was so funny
he wasn't wearing a jacket or shoes.
He was barefoot. And by funny I mean
disturbing. I've told this story thousands
of times, I hardly feel a thing. He'd jumped
out of a window, was what I found out
later, and fallen three stories without
breaking a bone. That night my mother cried
in my arms and said, This is a secret
we will take to our graves. I developed
innumerable compulsions, including
counting, hand-washing, scrupulosity
which is the fear that one has been sinful
in word or deed or thought. I was afraid
to leave the house, to touch any surface,
but I hid it so well that nobody
noticed. I was class president. I played
baseball, soccer. I wrote secret poetry.
And eventually I got out and went
to college. And things went coasting along
as well as things can in a family with
an inexplicably cruel father and
a masochistic mother who can't stop
talking about nothing. Logorrhea
is the clinical term, I think. Until
I came home one weekend for a visit
just before my wedding and my father
said I looked homeless. My beard and hair. When
in fact I looked just like other adjunct
professors of writing. But they told me
I looked like a man who'd slit his own throat.
There are things you don't know! I drove away
and haven't heard from them since. They are dead
to me.

Notes

THE BODY OF AN AMERICAN
by Dan O'Brien

The play had its European premiere at the Gate Theatre on 16 January 2014 in a co-production between the Gate Theare and Royal & Derngate in Northampton.

Mogadishu,1993. Dan is an American writer who is struggling to finish his play about ghosts. Paul is a Canadian photojournalist who is about to take a picture that will win him the Pulitzer Prize. Both men live worlds apart but a chance encounter over the airwaves sparks a special friendship. This play is a two-hander which sees two actors jump between more than thirty roles in a new form of documentary drama.

Here, Dan gives Paul a hard time about how dark he is and the fact that he always talks about death.

DAN – 30s (USA)

How can you live like that?
I mean, how can you walk around living
like you're going to die? Like back in LA
you can't be worried about the earthquake
that could erupt any second. You can't
ride the New York City subway thinking
about the likelihood of a terrorist
bomb exploding. Like on 9/11
I woke up –
                  And actually
I saw a ghost in our bedroom. Covered
in dust. Carrying his briefcase. He looked
so confused! He disappeared and I heard
the sirens. I went downstairs to find out
what was going on, and to hit Starbuck's
too. All these papers were spiraling down
from the sky. And I remember thinking
for a minute, Now all the bankers will
be humbled. I got my venti latte
and came back out in time to see the plane
hit the second tower. An old woman
sat down on the pavement and just started
sobbing. I went upstairs to get my wife

Notes

though we weren't married yet, and we joined
a river of people like refugees
walking uptown. While all the working men
and women were jumping. I never saw
my brother jump out the window. Maybe
there's something in that? A radio outside
a hardware store in Chinatown told us
the South Tower had come down. In a bar
somewhere in the East Village we watched as
the North Tower sank out of the blue sky
on TV. People were almost giddy
with panic, and grief. Some guys were tossing
a Frisbee in the street. I told myself,
If there's going to be a war, I will go.
I saw myself holding a machine gun
in my mind's eye, someplace bright and sandy
like Afghanistan, or maybe Iraq.
But I didn't go. Because I didn't
consider it the right war. Or because
nobody made me.

Notes

LITTLE LIGHT
by Alice Birch

Little Light *was first performed at the Orange Tree Theatre, Richmond on 4 February 2015.*

Married couple Alison and Teddy live by the sea. They are hosting the annual family dinner for Alison's estranged pregnant sister and her partner Simon. What unfolds is an evening of spats, marital dysfunction, seduction and revelations.

At dinner, Simon, who works in A&E, honestly describes how he often feels a mix of frustration, pain and empathy for his patients, who sometimes die, and how hard it is to detach himself, when he returns home to his pregnant girlfriend.

SIMON – LATE 30s* (UK)

When I first started A&E Rotations – and I was young, okay, I was really fucking new at life – it hadn't been hard yet – there was this ninety-year-old man. Something like my third day there and no one came to visit him. No one. And I couldn't believe it, I couldn't get my – I was cursing his relatives every time I passed his bed, which happened more and more because I couldn't stand how alone he was and my own Granddad had died a few weeks before this and we'd all just fucking Crammed in to get a second with him.

He died, this man – he died and still nobody came. His face was very very grey. Covered in lines, he looked like a child had sort of. Scribbled across his face. But. I remembered his hands – one was underneath his body and the other sort of reached out a little. I remember – or, no, okay, I remember Thinking that his his fingers were shaped into the form of some other hand that wasn't there.

There were bits of of dried blood around his eyes. I don't know why it hadn't come off but it looked like someone had drawn a pair of glasses in black marker pen. Sort of made you want to laugh. Think I did.

---

* *Older in the play but can be played younger.*

Notes

His back was broken. His spine snapped. His bones stuck out at funny angles.

And. I couldn't fit him together. He was in pieces. I remember putting my hand into his. I remember trying to make him a whole, vivid being.

He had been pushed in his wheelchair from a balcony on the tenth storey of a high-rise flat.

.

I was Obsessed. With the details.

I Howled.

He had been alone and it was That Hand.

.

His grandson had pushed him. He had abused his twenty-five-year-old grandson for the first fourteen years of that boy's life and he'd just

Snapped.

Lost it and pushed him. Or maybe he planned it and just pushed him, I don't know.

And. I felt this enormous betrayal. Because.

I'd sat with him as he died, this old old man and made him into something and had had Felt for him, I'd truly felt for him and Grieved for him

But also for that empty room. And grieved for some fear in me – a fear that my room would be as still.

I was Livid.

And and distraught and.

That was it. It's easy – it is instinct to reach out and to kill your own life for another's loss – it feels human, it feels natural, the way that it ought to be.

Of course it is difficult to detach. To go home and kiss your pregnant girlfriend and her bump and feel this this warmth of your own life's constancy and forget the people whose lives have just changed beyond all recognition in front of you. All of these lives hanging onto this thread, this this deeply Unnatural thread and all thoughts and memories and futures from that moment onwards blurred.

It took me years to forget his name.

Notes

LITTLE LIGHT
by Alice Birch

Little Light *was first performed at the Orange Tree Theatre, Richmond on 4 February 2015.*

Married couple Alison and Teddy live by the sea. They are hosting the annual family dinner for Alison's estranged pregnant sister and her partner Simon. What unfolds is an evening of spats, marital dysfunction, seduction and revelations.

This has been edited from a much longer speech which comes at the end of the play. Here, Teddy's hands are covered in plaster and blood as he has just demolished a wall to the surprise of his wife as he painfully recounts the loss of their child.

TEDDY – 30s (UK)

I haven't really slept.

In three days.

Maybe four.

I've tried shutting my eyes. But it's like I can't. Physically do it.

Three days.

It's ten years ago and it's two o'clock in the morning and I'm having a bath and I've finished all my marking and I want a bath to stop my bones from dropping out to keep my eyes open and I'm having a bath to put myself back together. And you have on this dress, this light light dress that pulls in at your waist and falls low on your back and all of your hair is up on your lovely head and the whole room is steam.

I'm in the bath. And you're stepping out of the dress and into the bath all at once and I want to hold your hands that are on your little stomach as you tell me. Your bright bare shoulders and your beam from the very middle of you as you tell me and I hold all of you. I hold your head and your back and your stomach and your arms in one go and everything that I had hoped for is contained, locked in you and your stomach.

And then it was six years ago.

These big, proud, round letters on leather handbags and around skirting boards and staircases in purple crayon.

Notes

And she's loud. She sings. She sits on my shoulders and she's funny. She's the funniest person that I have ever met. I have a new name. A short name that smacks of something happy

And she's happy and she's big and she's filling rooms in a house and we are one two three happy.

And then.

It's five years ago and she's gone.

I find a purple crayon Molly in tiny letters behind the fridge and I can't stand up for a week.

And it's four years ago and I can't remember.

Her weight written as a number and her shoes that we keep in the cupboard in her room that wouldn't fit her anymore and her funny little smell and the knowledge that she loved Ribena and the photographs of her that we keep in drawers for your self-preservation won't combine to create anything real.

She's lost. And seems to be found only in radio waves and television reports that are less frequent now, less supportive now, less there now.

And you're gone.

And. This year. This year is different.

I can't sleep.

And you've left you've gone and I think you've left notes there's so much more that

I'm supposed to Do this year. I have to make something I have to make the lunch but it's too dark I can't find anything. I know it's the same – I know that everything must be as it always is and I know that you think this is the biggest way to say I love you now. I love you now. I love you now. I love you now. Doesn't mean as much on such well-practised lips.

Four days ago and you've gone.

And the phone won't stop screaming.

And the birds won't stop ringing.

Notes

GNIT
by Will Eno

The play was first performed on 15 March 2013 at the Actors Theatre of Louisville by special arrangement with Signature Theatre and United Talent Agency.

Gnit is a 'fairly rough translation' of Henrik Ibsen's 19th-century Norwegian play Peer Gynt. *Peter is a foolhardy, ambitious, self-deluded anti-hero. He steals a bride on her wedding day and ends up banished from his town.*

This speech comes in Act 4 when Peter is older. He's at a seaside bar in Morocco. The barman asks him 'What's new?'.

This speech doesn't have to be done with an American accent.

PETER – LATE 30s* (USA)

Oh, Jesus, let's see. Went to a wedding a bunch of years ago, met this great woman Solvay, then ran off with the bride but changed my mind, and I had to leave town and these people sued my mother, and then I got lost and had a run-in with these crazy people – realtors, I guess – impregnated one, supposedly, then met up with something called "the middle," that was challenging, then built a little house, got back together with the great woman from the wedding, but the realtoress – who turned out to be a magical witch or had gotten sick or something – came around with my so-called son, and that ruined that, so then I had to leave again. These last few years, on the look-out for my true self, I got into the baby trade, sold plots of fake land, formed a little church, a strictly paper-based sort of thing, got very wealthy, met some more women, had a string of really successful relationships. Before that, mom went blind and died, that was hard. She was an angel, in retrospect. I left before the funeral, I don't know why, it was a confusing time – I trust she got buried all right. We always do, eventually. Then I did some more shit, tried to make some people pay for my mother's death and my dad's life, ugly stuff, nothing you'd really put on the resumé. Anyway, now I'm here: Sunny Morocco! I'm hoping to get into

* *The full age range for this role is 30s-50's.*

Notes

some arms dealing, some really serious money, as I'd like to be even richer, as I've got this massive inferiority-complex, or, this tiny superiority-complex. I'm standing here right now, with my life in a bag, all my money in a bag, no reason to look back, nothing to look back at. I'm staring at you, and, I want to be the fucking Emperor.

Notes

CADRE
by Omphile Molusi

The play premiered in the UK on 29 July 2013 at the Traverse Theatre, Edinburgh. It was produced by Chicago Shakespeare Theater and Richard Jordan Productions Ltd in association with The Market Theatre of Johannesburg, Traverse Theatre, and Adelaide Festival of Arts.

Cadre *was written in honour of the 21,000 who died during apartheid and all the thousands of unreported and unrecorded deaths of that time. It explores the journey of a young activist, Gregory, in apartheid South Africa. The play ranges from the 1960s until the fall of Apartheid in 1994, showing stories of the protagonist's personal and political journey. Gregory struggles to make sense of his life and navigate his way through a tumultuous political landscape.*

This speech comes towards the end of the play; Gregory is with the girl he likes, Sasa, and he's giving evidence to Colonel Botha at the Mmabatho police station conference/interrogation room.

GREGORY – 30s (BLACK/SOUTH AFRICAN)

My ears were open at all times. This information I would pass on to Cadres underground on a daily basis. The Colonel was determined to get us all into prison. I was determined to get everyone out of prison. He put roadblocks everywhere around the Botswana border where Cadres were coming in from military training into the country. I was there listening ... passing on information to my Commanders.

I couldn't let anyone get arrested. No leader was arrested on my watch. Crocodile Junior Botha was not happy at all. He was not catching the big fishes. This made him very suspicious.

In times of war ... there's never time to think. What was done was done. I had to get to him before he got to me.

How do you prepare for the unknown? I guess in a time of war ... even the prepared are always caught off-guard. The Crocodile sent me to the interrogation room and said he was coming back. There was a woman waiting to be interrogated. *(Sasa enters and sits on the bench with her head down.)* I had never walked into the interrogation room without Crocodile Junior Botha. I kept thinking ... what was he thinking ...? I always

Notes

wanted to know ... I wanted to crawl into his head and read his mind ... It was my duty to know ... so I can be ten steps ahead of him. But on this day ... I never knew what I was walking into.

Sorry, Mama. Just to prepare you. There's a white man who is going to walk in here. He is going to ask me to beat you up or he might ask me to do something even worse to you. It all depends on what you've been accused of. I am very sorry, but I will not have a choice but to beat you up. (*He takes out a belt.*) But if you survive this interrogation ... I will personally make sure that you escape. Say anything to him ... give him misleading information.

That was a bloody war! I couldn't just sit by and ... That was a situation that could only be changed by the direct intervention of the people themselves, come what may! And we almost did it. I am a soldier. I am a Cadre. I will not run anymore. Soldiers die but the cause lives on. The struggle continues?

Notes

PETER AND ALICE
by John Logan

Peter and Alice *by John Logan was first performed in London on 9th March 2013 at the Noël Coward Theatre as part of the Michael Grandage Company Season of five plays.*

The play depicts the real-life inspirations for Lewis Carroll's Alice in Wonderland *and JM Barrie's* Peter Pan *in the form of 80-year-old Alice Liddell Hargreaves and 30-year-old Peter Llewelyn Davies who met in a London bookshop in 1932, at the opening of a Lewis Carroll exhibition.*

The play is set in the backroom of the Bumpus bookshop in London on June 26, 1932.

In this speech Peter painfully reminisces to Alice about his traumatic time during and after the First World War.

PETER – 30s (UK)

Once the war came, everything you thought you knew ...

One day I killed a man, you see. In the deep, dark woods. The forest was choked up with bodies and mud. I was knee deep in it. If you step on a body you can split the stomach and release the gasses, and the stench is appalling, so I was looking down, trying not to step on any corpses, I looked up and the fellow was suddenly just there in front of me and I shot him ...

I didn't even know if he was a German, his uniform was so muddy. I just shot him in the chest. I was so scared ... I sat down on the ground and watched him die. I knew he was dead when he didn't move, but the fleas did. They crawled away from him, like they knew, like they were abandoning him, it was so sad ... I sat on the ground and I watched him die ... Then I went mad.

Shell-shock they call it, but it wasn't a shock. <u>It was a numbing</u>. I felt absolutely nothing as my life cracked open and spilled out of my head, started pooling around my feet ... I was seconded home, in shame. I went to asylums. Light bulb never off: suicide watch. Rubber mouth guard so I wouldn't bite my tongue off ... But my life was still pooling around my feet. I couldn't stop it. I was all cracked open.

Notes

Maybe there was a time but ... The war ditched me really, and then Michael's death. The nightmares are pretty unspeakable. You see, when I close my eyes I see them, my family ... and I feel ... <u>I feel they are waiting for me</u>. As if I would be <u>betraying</u> them if I didn't join them: for we are a family defined by our sadness ... To this day I'm frightened to close my eyes, because when I do I see them, that line of corpses, lunging for me in the dark ... My father, gaping in that monstrous leather jaw ... My mother, falling in the parlor, hand outstretched ... My brother George, bloody hands gripping the barbed wire tight ... My brother Michael, eyes staring up, sinking down, reaching for me ... I see them ... Even now ... <u>even now</u>.

Notes

MOSCOW STATIONS
by Venedikt Erofeev
Adapted by Stephen Mulrine

Moscow Stations *was commissioned by the Traverse Theatre, Edinburgh, and first produced on BBC Radio 3 in 1992. The first stage production, was at the Traverse Theatre 1993. This production transferred to the Garrick Theatre, London, in 1994, and to the Union Square Theater, New York, the following year.*

A novel adapted into a tour de force one-man play featuring Venichka Erofeev (Venya) – a cultured alcoholic, self-mocking intellectual, who regales us with an account of his 'heroic' odyssey from Moscow to provincial Petushki. This speech is taken from the beginning of the play when he's staggering through the streets of Moscow.

The speech doesn't have to be done with a Russian accent.

VENICHKA (VENYA) – 30s (RUSSIAN)

Everybody says: 'the Kremlin, the Kremlin.' They all go on about it, but I've never seen it. The number of times I've been drunk or hung over, traipsing round Moscow from one end to the other, and I've never once seen the Kremlin. For instance, yesterday – yesterday I didn't see it again, and it's not that I was particularly drunk. I mean, as soon as I came out onto Savyelov Station, I had a glass of Zubrovka for starters, 'cause I know from experience that as an early morning tipple, nobody's so far dreamed up anything better.

Anyway, a glass of Zubrovka. Then after that – on Kalyaev Street – another glass, only not Zubrovka this time, but coriander vodka. A friend of mine used to say coriander had a dehumanizing effect on a person, i.e., it refreshes your parts but it weakens your spirit. For some reason or other it had the opposite effect on me, i.e., my spirit was refreshed, while my parts went all to hell. But I do agree it's dehumanizing, so that's why I topped it up with two glasses of Zhiguli beer, plus some egg-nog out the bottle, in the middle of Kalyaev Street.

Of course, you're saying: come on, Venya, get on with it – what did you have next? And I don't know exactly. I remember I had two glasses of Hunter's vodka, on Chekhov Street. But I couldn't have made it across the ring road with nothing to drink. I really couldn't. So I must've had something else.

30s
168/169

Notes

Anyway, after that I walked into the city centre, 'cause whenever I'm looking for the Kremlin, I invariably end up at Kursk Station. I mean, I was supposed to go to Kursk Station, and not into the city centre, but I made for the centre regardless, to have a look at the Kremlin even just once. I knew I wouldn't find it. I knew I'd end up at Kursk Station.

I'm so annoyed now I could almost cry. And it's not because I didn't make it to Kursk Station, or because I woke up this morning in some godforsaken entry. (I'd sat down on the entry step, pressed my little suitcase to my heart, and fallen asleep just like that.) No, what's bugging me is this: I've just worked it out, that from Chekhov Street up to that entry I must've drunk more than six roubles' worth – but of what, and where? And in what order? And did drinking it do me any good? Nobody knows, and nobody'll ever know. I mean, to this day we don't know whether Tsar Boris killed the Crown Prince Dmitri, or the other way round.

Anyway, when I came out this morning into the fresh air it was already dawn. And if you've ever fetched up unconscious in some entry, and emerged from it at dawn, well, you'll know what a heavy heart I bore down the forty steps of that godforsaken place.

If you want to go left, Venya, then go left, I'm not forcing you to do anything. If you want to go right, go right. Just wrap up against the wind and go quietly. And breathe only when you've got to. Breathe so your feet don't keep grazing the back of your knees ...

I'd better find a pillar to lean against, and shut my eyes tight, so I won't feel so sick ...

Notes

PASTORAL

by Thomas Eccleshare

The first preview of Pastoral *was at Soho Theatre on 25 April 2013. The play had its world premiere on 2 May 2013 at the HighTide Festival.*

Pastoral is set in an England where nature has gobbled up the high street and an old woman named Moll waits in her flat for the Ocado man. In this speech we hear the lengths to which this Ocado man has gone, in order to complete his delivery, no matter how treacherous a journey.

OCADO MAN – 30s* (UK)

I was attacked. My van was useless, stuck in a bog, stuck in Parson's Road. I left it there you see. I set out on foot. I got told, Mr. Sanderson told me, another complaint from a customer, another missed order, and I was liable to get the sack. To get fired. It's actually quite a responsibility when you think of it. I'm an ambassador. So it's up to me to provide the goods, to get them to the address. Well, that's why I set out on foot. It was alright at first. Headed down Alders Way, towards the Corn Exchange. I'd planned to nip round the back of the Odeon and come at you that way. I'd say it was almost pretty. Quite idyllic actually. There's no road anymore, but it's not like this yet. There's little saplings, bushes and reeds. The edge of Copling Street's fallen in and got filled in with rain water. There's all sorts there now, it's like a stream, trickling down the hill. Frogs, toads, beavers, fish. Dragonflies as big as my finger. And the birds! Ducks and geese and swans everywhere. Others that I don't know the names of, great big ones overhead, little ones twitching their heads at me. I stopped and had a paddle. That's where I lost my shoes. A little fox came and nicked them when I was paddling. So I pushed off from the pond barefoot. Still had all the bags at this point: Fridge, cupboard, freezer. Packed full. Oh, the stuff I had for you in those bags. I mean, you'll know, you ordered it but, oh the glory! Oh lord! There was cooked hams and cured meats, diced chicken and ready-to-eat veg. I had olives for

---

* *The character could be of any age.*

Notes

the oldies, and Fabs for the little ones. Crisps and chocolate and cereals and coffee. In the cupboard bag, I had a plastic box full of mini doughnuts. Each one was like a perfect wheel, dusted with icing sugar, delicate as snow. I tasted one. I know I shouldn't have but I got so hungry on the journey. I tasted one and – oh – it was soft, so soft, and the sugar fell into my mouth as if the very air had been sweetened. I let the dough dissolve in my mouth, I let my saliva sit with it, let it soak until I had to swallow the whole thing down.

They got me outside Habitat. It was forest by that point. So dark and dense, like this. There was barely anything left of the shop, but I could see the remains of sofas, stuck in the branches of a birch. An armchair, right up high, with a warbling robin nesting in its back. They ripped the food from the bags, even the frozen stuff. They knocked me to the ground and kicked and bit and scratched me. I tried to hold on. I thought about what Mr. Sanderson would say when I got back to the depot. I knew it was the end, he'd throw me out on my ear. But they were too strong, too many. They ate in front of my face. They gobbled it down like wolves. They crammed the fruit and veg into their hungry mouths. They tore open the bagels and the pitta bread and ate them in two bites. They moaned and growled in ecstasy. And they fed their young with the crisps and the raw meat. The milk ran down their throats and down their necks in great rivers, sticky and thick. Crème fraiche, pork pies, oven pizzas, gone. And when they had finished, when there was not so much as a puff of dusty sugar left in the air, they left me, face down in the earth, my wrist sprained, my nose bloodied. I didn't know what else to do, so I went on. And I did it. I made it here. And I saved something. I did manage to save something.

Notes

KHANDAN (FAMILY)

by Gurpreet Kaur Bhatti

Commissioned by Birmingham Repertory Theatre and first performed at The STUDIO, Birmingham Repertory Theatre on 22 May 2014. The production then transferred to the Royal Court Theatre, London, on 11 June 2014.

The play deals with the trials and tribulations of a British Asian family – their relationships, tensions and dysfunctions. The mother is a widow who has spent her life working hard and making sacrifices for her children. All she wants to do is go back to her homeland Punjab.

Pal Gill, her son, is described as a 'powerfully built leonine alpha male, ridden with ambition.' He's got big plans for his daddy's business and speaks his mind to his mother.

PAL – EARLY 30s (BRITISH ASIAN)

Daddy died because he drank too much.

Every night he'd sip his Bacardi bottle till the room started to spin. Then he'd start crying and want a hug and start singing *(Sings.)* 'Peenee peenee peenee peenee eh sharab.' *['Drink, drink, drink booze.']* An hour later you'd be walking around with a bucket of Dettol, mopping up his sick and piss.

I'd come home from school with a love bite or homework or bruises on my face and you'd be stuck in that stock room counting tins of beans. You never bothered to talk to me or Cookie.

I didn't ask for any of it Mum. You just thought I wanted what you wanted. But you never asked me. I could have taken exams, gone to college even …

If I hadn't spent every school night behind that till the results might have been better. You never paid any attention to what I was capable of. I could be working in the City now. Making a fortune …

Daddy never gave me no power. I took it. He would have done the same.

I'm building a nursing home. With Harj. We've been talking about it for months. Been to the bank with the business plan and they've said yes. We're gonna renovate a pub. The King

Notes

George. Daddy used to go there on a Friday night when we were kids. Remember? It's like a cemetery now. We're starting small but we know what we want. There's a load of money in care homes Mum. I can do this. I want to show you ...

Notes

ZHE: [NOUN] UNDEFINED

by Chuck Mike, Antonia Kemi Coker
and Tonderai Munyevu

The play premiered in the UK on 10 October 2013 at the Burton Taylor Studio, Oxford Playhouse in Oxford.

ZHE' (pronounced zee) is a gender-neutral pronoun – not he or she.

This two-hander play deals with growing up and self-discovery. A Zimbabwean boy comes to London when he is thirteen years old and discovers his sexuality. His family and childhood bullies have all shaped him to the man he is today.

Here he is opening up to the 'Woman' about his boarding school days.

MAN – 30 (GAY/BLACK/SOUTH AFRICAN)

It was a Catholic Missionary School; so, slowly, I became very religious, and yet ... sensually awakened all at the same time. For my school uniform I wore a blue shirt, striped blue and white tie, grey shorts, long grey stockings and black shoes. In the winter we would add long grey trousers, blue woollen sweaters and for me, a very long, custom-made scarf, naturally I added a layer of thick soles to my black shoes to give me a little extra height – actually an extra strut. Everyone loved me. They'd talk about 'ngochani'[1], I didn't know what that meant. I had never heard *it* mentioned — I never considered *it* — I remember my grandmother when I was growing up saying 'Pane nyaya, you're not going to be doing any of *that** but she never told me what 'that' was – and clearly she knew what I was. In school there was a disco every Saturday ... hormones raging, the generator overworked would shut down and the lights would go off. The rules said you needed to go to your dormitories and sleep ... I remember getting to my dormitory, I actually took it all seriously – 'oh the lights have gone off, I guess we have to go to bed'... So I got into my bed and slept. And then, like five minutes later, I sort of felt this movement at the bottom of my bed. Sort of like a hand coming through. And then like a person, and I thought 'Oh that's strange there is a person in my bed'. And then I recall smelling this person. I've never been that close to someone physically to smell them. I remember thinking that's a different scent, that's

Notes

how people smell when they are close to you. But I actually didn't know who this person was. I had no idea. And he just sort of, at first he lay down next to me and then I just sort of tried to respond. But I didn't know exactly what was going on. I remember there was no kissing. I just remember my body being moved and I didn't know what to do back so I just sort of allowed myself to move with whatever was happening. Then two minutes later – wetness – and that was it. And then he left just as inconspicuously as he'd come. It was like a memory, a distant – but real memory. Subsequently, I thought who was this person? And why me? What signal did I send off. And then I got used to it. I got used to it. On occasions I crept into other peoples' beds too, sometimes with my heart in my mouth 'cause you don't want to creep into some macho man's bed.

[1] Shona expression for homosexual

This line is spoken by Grandma in the original playtext. Here, I'm suggesting including it as part of the monologue.

Notes

ZHE: [NOUN] UNDEFINED
by Chuck Mike, Antonia Kemi Coker
and Tonderai Munyevu

The play premiered in the UK on 10 October 2013 at the Burton Taylor Studio, Oxford Playhouse in Oxford.

ZHE' (pronounced zee) is a gender-neutral pronoun – not he or she.

This two-hander play deals with growing up and self-discovery. A Zimbabwean boy comes to London when he is 13 years old and discovers his sexuality. His family and childhood bullies have all shaped him to the man he is today.

Here he is opening up to the 'Woman' about his adulthood.

MAN – 30 (GAY/BLACK/SOUTH AFRICAN)

My faith was withering. I went to university to study theology and I came out with a passion for acting. In my mind I became sort of invisible. Even in a gay bar I didn't tick any boxes. I wasn't a 'bear'[1] or a 'cub'[2] or even a 'twink'[3]. I was just indefinable. A grey cloud sunk into me. I partied hard. As long as it kept me up I would take it. I became reckless. Truth is, the more drugs and alcohol I took the harder it was to forget. The thing about coke is that it takes the glint, the sparkle in your eyes away from you and before you know it, you have forgotten how to genuinely smile. I wanted to have sex and walk away. Strangers wouldn't ask questions about my body — I wanted to forget – it didn't matter when, where or how, I just really wanted somebody, I didn't care — if he wanted me, I would be up for it — just the thrill of being touched. Gay, guy sex can be rough and I was ready for anything — it was frightening. It all came to a head one night after a long binge of coke and vodka in Soho. I staggered up to the square park and saw a few men having sex. I managed to sneak in by jumping the fence and walked around the park. I found a guy. I didn't care that he wasn't good looking, if he wanted me, I was happy for him to do whatever he wanted me to do. He came to me and started kissing me. We started having sex, the kind you have in a park, that is not very comfortable. My phone rang, I recognized the ringtone and reached into my pocket but could not find it, I checked every other pocket and I still could not find it and I finally realized that this guy, who was fucking me, had stolen my phone. I asked for it back and

Notes

continued to have sex with him. I didn't ask why he had stolen my phone. I didn't care. I just wanted the sex to continue because I felt that's what I needed. Someone having sex with me. From the distance I could hear a police siren approaching and people in the park scattering and jumping the fence to get away. The guy I was with suddenly came on me and he too scattered, with an agility of someone used to running away from trouble. I was too drunk, too high and at this stage in too much physical pain from sex to actually run away. The police car arrived, lights flashing. It was clear that the policeman was pretending he hadn't seen me to give me time to climb the fence and make a getaway. I couldn't. I was too drunk. I struggled to jump that fence and the policeman averted his gaze once more. I tried again, I couldn't. I got stuck at the top of the fence. The lights were bright. Spotlighting me. Eventually I fell to the ground and slowly, painfully made my way home. When I woke up the next day –

I realized something had to change.

[1] Hairy, muscular or stocky, masculine type

[2] Younger version of bear

[3] Usually under 30, without hair, effeminate looking

Notes

THE BARDS OF BROMLEY
by Perry Pontac

The play was broadcast on BBC Radio 4 in 2004.

The Bards of Bromley *is the first meeting of a writers' workshop, attended by a group of unusually promising authors: William Wordsworth, George Eliot, August Strindberg, A A Milne and Johann Wolfgang von Goethe.*

Here, Strindberg is addressing and critiquing Wordsworth, the poet.

This speech doesn't have to be done with a Swedish accent.

AUGUST STRINDBERG – 30s (SWEDISH)

My dear Wordsworth, please consider: Your beloved daffodils, far from being blameless ornaments of nature, are the tumours of the earth – vile excrescences rising unbidden, posturing like prostitutes, flaunting their bodies, sending their stink abroad, luring the callow bees into their rank entrails. All flowers – daffodils, the noxious buttercup, the sinister periwinkle – are nourished by rotting corpses and the worms that feed on them, blind and voracious gluttons, grubs and slugs and things of slime. *And* the working classes – they play their part in it somehow, I assure you.

Ignore it if you will, Wordsworth, but daffodils, like all plants, are a plague and a parasite on man, sprouting and festering in the cracks and corners of life. I would kill all flowers – raze them like invading troops. And trees as well. What are they but gigantic weeds, giving shelter and succour to birds with their idiotic cries and filthy personal habits? No, death to all vegetation, all verdure, all foliage, all growth. Give me honest sterility, the dead promise of a barren field.

Embrace the bleakness in life, man. Court the horror. Only then will freedom come, the freedom of disgust!

And as for wandering 'lonely as a cloud' – my play *The Dance of Death* is about true loneliness, the loneliness of a man surrounded by family and friends. And there is loneliness in my *Miss Julie*, *The Ghost Sonata* and *The Dream Play*. Did you steal the theme of loneliness from me? It seems an extraordinary coincidence.

'Lonely as a cloud.' 'Lonely as a cloud'? What a ridiculous

Notes

conceit. A cloud is not lonely. It is also not happy, or indignant, or easily embarrassed, or secretly amused. A cloud is a phenomenon of nature – and is therefore wicked, malevolent, cunning, a curse on man and an engine thwarting his every design.

And, like the English month, I have my bright periods as well as my occasional thundery showers. Moments of wild ecstasy and violent rage, sudden fainting fits, days of crippling doubt, months of arrogant certainty – I've known them all.

Notes

THE DEAD WAIT
by Paul Herzberg

The Dead Wait *was first performed at The Market Theatre, Johannesburg in 1997, having been shortlisted for The Verity Bargate Award. It was then produced at The Royal Exchange in 2002, It had its London premiere in 2013 at Park 200 in a revised version.*

Based on a true story, it is an explosive journey through war, death and redemption, following three people caught in the insanity of conflict and haunted by its horrors.

Twenty years earlier, Josh was a conscript in the South African army. He is talking to Lily Jozana, daughter of George Jozana, political exile and Brigadier in the armed wing of the African National Congress. Lily has returned to South Africa having spent her youth in exile. Josh is attempting to explain to her the circumstances of her father's death.

JOSH GILMORE – LATE 30s (WHITE/SOUTH AFRICAN)

I've ... always known where you were. I kept track of you. We lived near each other in London for many years. When you finally returned so long after the elections, it felt very strange.

Pause.

I know ... it must be the hardest thing you've ever done, listening to that story. I tried to explain ... cover as much as I could. I'm sure I failed. But then my life ...

LILY does not respond. JOSH starts to hyperventilate. He remembers to breathe into his jacket and starts to calm down.

I was acting under orders. That's not an excuse. I simply didn't have the courage to disobey. I'm not asking for forgiveness. How could you grant it? All I can do is express my remorse, my sorrow and ... *shame* for what happened to your father — *Jesus, how useless is language.*

Pause.

You ask what I want. I want ... some kind of justice.

Pause.

A month after it happened the war ended. And Papa Louw vanished. If I find him there may be little that can be done

Notes

officially as the crime was committed on foreign soil. And of course the truth commission no longer exists. And the country no longer seems to have the appetite. *But I intend to force him out from under his rock.*

Pause.

I do know something about you. I know he loved you.

Pause.

You say you came for your family. That the pain of the families of the dead is not knowing. Then I must answer to all the Jozanas.

Pause.

Sixty kilometres north of Ondangwa on the Namibian border are the Naulila Falls. If you stand with your back to them, facing north, you'll see a hillock sticking out of the earth, about the height of a man.

(Pause.)

I shot your father at the base of that hillock.

Notes

The Plays

Bottleneck
Luke Barnes
9781849434379

**The Keepers of
Infinite Space**
Omar El-Khairy
9781783190768

**Some People Talk
About Violence**
Lulu Raczka,
Barrel Organ
9781783199648

Chalk Farm
AJ Taudevin,
Kieran Hurley
9781783190218

Violence and Son
Gary Owen
9781783198931

Whole
Philip Osment
9781849434454

Solomon and Marion
Lara Foot Newton
9781849435079

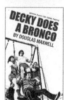

**Decky Does
a Bronco**
Douglas Maxwell
9781840022438

Too Fast
Douglas Maxwell
9781849431255

Velocity
Daniel MacDonald
9781783191475

Fear of Music
from *What You
Wish For In Youth*
Barney Norris
9781783199174

Wise Guys
from *Osment: Plays
for Young People*
Philip Osment
9781840022728

The Saints
Luke Barnes
9781783191550

Lungs
Duncan Macmillan
9781849431453

Carthage
Chris Thompson
9781783190690

Pineapple
from *The Oberon
Anthology of
Contemporary Irish Plays*
Phillip McMahon
9781849433914

Perfect Match
Gary Owen
9781783190607

Innocence
from *Dea Loher:
Three Plays*
Dea Doher
9781783190621

Eventide
Barney Norris
9781783199112

Operation Crucible
Kieran Knowles
9781783190805

Chapel Street
Luke Barnes
9781849434263

RED
John Logan
9781840029444

**The Well and
Badly Loved**
Ben Webb
9781849431705

**The Body of
an American**
Dan O'Brien
9781783190911

Little Light
Alice Birch
9781783192090

Gnit
Will Eno
9781783190294

Cadre
Omphile Molusi
9781783190454

Peter and Alice
John Logan
9781849434744

Moscow Stations
Venedikt Erofeev
translated by
Stephen Mulrine
9781783191321

Pastoral
Thomas Eccleshare
9781849434447

Khandan (Family)
Gurpreet Kaur Bhatti
9781783190935

Zhe: [noun] Undefined
Chuck Mike,
Antonia Kemi Coker,
Tonderai Munyevu
9781783190720

**The Bards of
Bromley and
Other Plays**
Perry Pontac
9781849434270

The Dead Wait
Paul Herzberg
9781840023428